CONTENTS

1	Fate Disguised As A Thief	Pg 1
2	Arrival In Fez	Pg 11
3	Working At The Center	Pg 22
4	On The Road Again	Pg 45
5	Changing Of The Guard	Pg 55
6	To Oregon And Back	Pg 62
7	Chefchaouen	Pg 67
8	Casablanca	Pg 75
9	Marrakesh and the South	Pg 78
10	The Export Biz	Pg 86
11	The Shawafa	Pg 95
12	Meknes	Pg 109
13	Fez Apartment	Pg 128
14	Moroccan Weddings	Pg 137
15	Fate Disguised As A Raffle	Pg 148
16	Paintings By The Author	Pg 183
17	About The Author & Editor	Pg 198
18	Acknowledgements	Pg 199
18	Glossary	Pg 200

1 - FATE DISGUISED AS A THIEF

My first sight of Morocco came at dusk in September of 1971. I was aboard a twenty-three-foot trimaran named *Carnival*, sailing along Spain's Mediterranean coast with three friends. We had come from the northern Spanish island Formentera, and we were sailing to Gibraltar. I was just twenty-two and had never been sailing before, let alone at sea. The previous night, there had been a horrendous easterly storm with huge swells that I was sure would snap the boat in two. (A trimaran is as wide as it is long with a main hull and two small outrigger hulls on each side attached only by lateral fiberglass beams.) The swells would raise one side of the boat, then bring it crashing down with a loud unnerving bang. Anyone who thinks the 'Med' is a pussycat hasn't seen the lion roar in September. I prayed to God that if He would just get me safely back to land, I would never again take to sea in a small craft.

That night we sailed three times further than we had on the previous three days, so I was under the mistaken impression that the lights I was seeing in the distance were just Spanish fishing boats and not the Moroccan coastline. It was only as day broke that I realized how far we had sailed during the night with the aid of the storm. Morocco was to our left, Gibraltar to our right.

As it turned out, we still had some serious sailing to do. Because the Strait of Gibraltar is a funnel where the Atlantic Ocean fills the Mediterranean Sea, some of the most powerful currents in the world move through the strait. We spent several hours sailing near the

Moroccan coast - unable to fight our way to Gibraltar's harbor.

I remember my surprise as we sat there. I had been under the mistaken impression that Morocco was all desert with an occasional oasis. However, its Mediterranean coastline was covered with pine and fir trees and reminded me of Marin County in the San Francisco Bay Area. Then in desperation, I tried tacking back in the direction from which we had come and illogically we were at last being carried off to Gibraltar.

You can't imagine our relief once inside the jetties of the Gibraltar harbor. We were all high fives, hugs, and kisses. We had made it alive - something that seemed unlikely on several occasions during the four-hundred-and-fifty-mile sail. We took down our sails and pulled into what appeared to be a vacant slot on the pier. However, once there we saw a small sign indicating that this spot was reserved for her Majesty's Royal Navy. We concluded that we best not start our stay in Gibraltar by upsetting Her Majesty.

Upon looking around the crowded pier, we saw another spot on the other side of the harbor. Since our sails were already down and our outboard motor had long since stopped providing its services, Captain Russ concluded that he needed only to swim over to the other spot, taking a line with him, and then pull the *Carnival* over by reeling in its tether.

It should have been a perfectly good plan. Russ was an experienced sailor, young, strong, and athletic. Unfortunately, the wind kicked up after Russ had pulled the *Carnival* about halfway. The *Carnival* began picking up speed and Russ' furious pulling couldn't prevent her from heading toward nearby boats. Talk about a helpless sinking feeling - we could only watch. However, at the last moment before crashing into a small boat I ran to the bow and jumped onto the boat we were about to crash into and pushed back at the *Carnival*. This sent me flying but fortunately I had slowed the *Carnival* sufficiently to avoid damage to either boat. Nonetheless, there still was a great bang and the boats rocked about wildly.

An instant later, a bearded young man appeared from inside the tiny boat, rubbing sleep from his eyes and looking completely disoriented. At that moment Mary Ann jumped down on his deck, stuck out her hand and said, "Hi, my name is Mary Ann, it is nice to meet you. You wouldn't have a cigarette, would you?"

The guy hesitantly shook her hand and replied, "I am Mike, perhaps next time you could call first." Everyone laughed and full introductions were made. Mike was a Canadian and he had just sailed his twenty-three foot 'bathtub' across the Atlantic from Nova Scotia – no small feat. We congratulated him and he replied, "Actually, it has been a pretty uneventful trip until you folks showed up."

Gibraltar is a small peninsula of only six square miles that protrudes off the Iberian Peninsula. While it is rather non-consequential, this little piece of real estate is steeped with history. In mythology it is the northern Pillar of Hercules. (Ceuta being the southern.) The Phoenicians capped it with silver to warn other sea going Mediterraneans that this was the outer limits of safe sailing and world powers have been fighting over it ever since.

The British took control of Gibraltar after Admiral Lord Nelson defeated the Spanish armada in 1805 A.D. Not surprisingly the Spanish would like it back and it continues to be a source of contention between the two countries. As a way of expressing their displeasure, the Spanish periodically block the border and travel to Gibraltar becomes highly problematic.

Of course, Gibraltar is famous for its rock, which is actually a jutting mountain of limestone. It was here in 771 A.D. that the Berber General Tarak Ibn Ziyad landed for the Moorish conquest of Spain. He lined up his army on the beach and set fire to their boats, thus ensuring their unwavering dedication in the battles ahead. Gibraltar is in fact named for him. *Jebel* is the Arabic word for mountain and Jebel Tarak was eventually anglicized to Gibraltar.

Today, Gibraltar is more famous for the Barbary apes that colonize the upper reaches of the rock and as a place where a British tourist, weary of Spanish cuisine, can get genuine fish and chips. John Lennon married Yoko Ono here, and it was in the same judge's chambers that I would later marry my wife Louise (a somewhat lesser-known point of history.)

Our sailing mates Russ and Marty were meeting other friends who would be their crew for an Atlantic crossing. Mary Ann and I went looking for a travel agency to book airline tickets to the States. However, as we approached a travel agency, we saw a large poster in the window of a photo from the Moroccan city Fez. Men in white gowns and red fezzes (the traditional tall cylinder like hats) were standing in front of a splendid white building with carved plaster Islamic designs, mosaic tile and a dark green tile roof. It was so beautiful that I thought to myself that this must be the shining city on the hill that we all dream of. One look and I knew that I had to go there - and after all Morocco was just seven miles across the strait. You could feel it - almost touch it. Instead of buying airline tickets to the U.S., we bought ferry tickets to Morocco.

The following day, Mary Ann and I boarded the ferry *Ibn Battuta*, named for the famed Andalusian explorer. It was an unforgettably beautiful sunny day. The Mediterranean and Spain were behind us, Morocco and the Atlantic lay ahead. A dozen dolphins escorted the ferry; it was one of those voyages that travelers live to experience.

While on board, I had my first encounters with some of the men in flowing white robes that I had seen in the Gibraltar travel agency poster. If there hadn't been so many, I might have concluded that they were some sort of gurus, perhaps devotees of a mysterious sect. I also noticed that many of the Moroccans were in brown or stripped brown and white gowns. Others were in Western clothing, some well-dressed, others looking rather seedy and dangerous. Likewise, the women displayed a wide variety of apparel. Some wore long gowns in various colors, their faces covered with black veils. The younger women were generally in slacks, some in tight jeans. I was struck by how attractive the Moroccans are with their olive toned complexions and dark eyes.

It wasn't very long before we approached the port at the Bay of Tangier; it would be an experience for which growing up in suburban Oregon had not well prepared me. After we cleared customs and proceeded along the pier, a flock of young hustlers descended upon us. There was no shaking them. Some were being friendly. Others were casting insults - both personal and cultural. All of them had something to offer - hotels, restaurants, drugs, sex, anything money could buy.

I decided that it would be best to commission one of them for a hotel, see if he could get rid of the others, then try to regroup our senses. I scanned the faces of the assembled pack and selected the one who was least threatening. Fortunately, my strategy worked, and the others quickly dispersed. We then followed our new guide out of the port and up the adjacent hill until we reached the narrow alleys of the old *kasbah* (walled fort/district). We began passing grimy little cafes and restaurants. Some of the artisan shops looked interesting, but I was far too overwhelmed to worry about shopping. I began to fear we would never return from these alleys.

Finally, our guide turned into a doorway with a badly painted sign indicating that it was a hotel. Inside, we ducked around a woman who was mopping the hallway. Her gauzy dress and pantaloons were wrapped around her waist, and she was bent over swabbing the floor with a mop that had no stick. This was a good sign. The place was old and a little decrepit, but it was clean.

We checked in at the desk. The room would cost the equivalent of two dollars - not a big commitment, even to people of our very modest means. Our guide told us that he would let us rest and come back in a few hours to take us to dinner. Once in our room, we were much relieved to be free of our guide and we started scheming how we might rid ourselves of him.

I went downstairs and asked the desk clerk about trains to Fez. He said that there just happened to be one at four o'clock. Tangier seemed to be closing in around us. I was hopeful that Fez, the 'shinning city on the hill' from the travel poster, would be more welcoming. We grabbed our bags, gave the desk clerk eight *dirhams* ($2), and headed for the train station. I imagine the desk clerk was thinking that it was a good thing that these Americans have money because they sure have a hard time making up their minds.

The train station was just a short walk away, but it was jam packed and an unmitigated zoo. All the hustlers who had been at the port were now working the train station. So were the gum sellers, the kids selling cigarettes one at a time, as well as the peanut and sunflower seed merchants. We somehow managed to wrestle ourselves into the mass of human flesh pressing its way to the ticket windows.

At the window, I had prepared myself to order our tickets in French. However, the clerk responded in Spanish. I speak just enough Spanish to understand that the clerk was telling me that this is Tangier, and they speak Spanish not French. Truth of the matter is that French is the second language of Morocco (Arabic being the official language), although Tangier was once a part of Spanish Morocco. He had me somewhat rattled, which I suspect was intentional. I would later learn that Moroccans in public positions usually speak five or six languages, certainly Arabic, French, and probably English. In any case, while I was struggling to communicate with him and get my change, an arm reached over my shoulder and wrestled my wallet away. Perhaps it was just cultural paranoia, but as I pursued him, I had the distinct impression that everyone stepped out of his path and into mine.

By the time I got out of the station, the thief was already fifty meters down the street. Nonetheless, being a former track star, I began to close on him quickly. Once I got within twenty meters of him, I suddenly realized that he knew where he was going, and I didn't. He was probably armed with a knife, and I had left Mary Ann alone in the den of thieves. I called off the chase and hurried back to the station.

Back at the station, Mary Ann and I assessed our predicament. My wallet had both our passports and all our money. All we had left were the two tickets to Fez and about $10. I questioned some fellow American tourists and discovered that there was an American consulate in Tangier, but as it was the weekend it wouldn't open for a couple of days. We thought we might try to sell our tickets and hang on somehow until the consulate opened.

Mary Ann said that she wanted to consult the *I Ching*, something she would do when she was having a hard time deciding what to do. The *I Ching* is an ancient Chinese book of divination. Some call it fortune telling but Mary Ann said that when properly used it was more a psychological tool for helping you reflect on whether your motives are sincere and your decision making is based on an objective understanding of the situation. She would shake three ancient Chinese coins, cast them on a table or floor and see how many came up heads and how many were tails. She did this six times. This random calculation was used to direct her to a page called a hexagram, which gave some little parable of Confusion advice. I found that the advice was generally interesting and often quite uncanny. Certainly, it was better than fortune cookies, because at least you didn't have to pay for the meal to get the advice.

Mary Ann sat cross-legged on the train station's floor, closed her eyes, and gently shook the three coins. Then she softly tossed them to the concrete floor from only six inches above. However, one of the coins landed on its edge and rolled off across the train station as though it had legs. I jumped up and ran after it. The coin was traveling across an empty section of the station, and I was able to catch up to it rather easily, but just as I caught up, it slipped into a very narrow deep slot in the floor and disappeared for eternity.

Hopes dimmed, I walked back to Mary Ann. She couldn't help

laughing at the sight of me losing out to this little hole in the floor.

"It would seem that we are having a particularly unlucky day, don't you think?" I complained.

"No" she said, "I just think our fate has been cast, *I Ching* or not."

We began approaching people waiting to purchase their train tickets to see if they might buy their tickets from us instead. For the most part, they treated us like we were pesky panhandlers but after a while a well-dressed young Moroccan guy stopped and looked over our tickets. He suggested that we might as well go on to Fez as there was an American Cultural Center there, where we could get consular help. In the meantime, we were welcome to sleep on the couches in his apartment. Given our alternatives, this sounded pretty good, and he did seem sincere.

Once on the train, I began to visit with our rescuer. His name was Mohammed, although he preferred to be called Momi. He was only nineteen years old but explained that he was in the manufacturing and export business. This all sounded rather impressive for someone his age, but he did have an air of sophistication.

As the train rumbled along, I had my first clear, studied look at this place called Morocco. My first thought was what a poor country it was. This gave me a sinking feeling as I realized that I was near penniless myself and at the bottom of a food chain that wasn't doing so well itself. I would have become more concerned about our survival prospects had I not become so mesmerized by something else I was seeing. We were now passing through countryside where life was more organic than I had ever seen. There was something about these men in their *djellabas* - the full-length hand-woven wool garments that are worn in the rural areas as well as some in the cities. It was as if my eyes were being massaged by the wool's texture and softness. The more I saw, the more my spirits picked up. My sense of adventure returned, and I became hopeful that everything would work out; I could relax.

Keenan, Kiki, and Mary Ann off the Moroccan coastline

Amazigh (Berber) Lady – by the author

More paintings by the author beginning on page 183

2 - ARRIVAL IN FEZ

After an exhausting day that included missing a vital train connection that added several hours to the trip, we finally reached Fez in the early morning. We jumped into one of the little red Fiat taxis that were lined up outside the station and rode the short distance to Momi's apartment, which was just off the main boulevard in the *Ville Nouvelle* (the newer part of Fez which was built by the French during colonialization). The boulevard was tree-lined with fountains and full of aimless young men smoking and talking. We climbed the three stories to Momi's apartment. He searched his pockets and finally found the key to the door. We then got the first of many surprises to come.

For one thing, it was not exactly Momi's apartment. More accurately it was his father's apartment. We were told however that his father would not be around for a while, so it was a convenient time for guests. The main room, called the *majlis*, (sitting room) had puffy banquettes lined all the way around the walls. Over in one corner, a nearly deaf and blind grandfather resided. Momi and his brother shared a room and his parents another. Grandfather seemed a little wary of us, but Momi's mother made us feel very welcome. The younger brother Driss was about seventeen and was happy to have somebody help him with his English. In fact, he studied English in the evenings at the American Language Center and said that he would be glad to take us down there when it opened in a couple of days. Mary Ann and I each had a banquette to ourselves on the side of the room opposite of grandfather. The banquettes were comfortable enough and we were more than grateful to be able to stretch out and get some sleep.

The next morning, we all got up and had a very pleasant breakfast of freshly baked thick, round whole grain Moroccan bread with a bean dip, Turkish coffee, and black olives. Afterwards, Momi said he had work to do and asked if we wouldn't mind giving him a hand. He explained that way he would finish early and have time to take us down to the old *medina*. (*medina* simply means city in Arabic but in this context the locals were referring to what Westerners often refer to as the *kasbah*.) Naturally that was fine with us, and Momi came out of his room with several cardboard boxes.

This was surprise number two. Momi 'manufactured' *keef* or hash pipes that he sold to head shops in New York and Amsterdam. Quite simply, they were the gaudiest, most awful looking things I had ever seen. First, he would take the traditional Moroccan *keef* pipe, which is made of a wood stem about eight inches long with a little red clay bowl at the end that has the shape of a plumbing joint, then he would wrap the stem in velvet and glue junk jewelry on it. Needless to say, this was not my career objective, but we were truly appreciative of the generosity that we had been shown. So, we reluctantly participated in his multinational manufacturing enterprise. It is a skill that I choose to leave off my resume.

That afternoon Momi announced that we had worked enough, and we got ready for the trip to the *medina*. My expectations were high. The poster of Fez at the Gibraltar travel agency had led me to believe that I was about to see something truly fantastic. We strolled down the boulevard to the district called *mellah*, which is Arabic for salt. According to some accounts, in less politically correct times salted heads were stuck on poles in the *mellah* to remind the population of the price of disobedience. The *mellah* is adjacent to one of the King's palaces and a large Jewish community had lived there under the King's protection up until the 1963 Arab-Israeli War when most of them migrated to Israel.

We continued a short distance and entered *bab al-batha*, one of the numerous gates to the walled *medina*. The atmosphere changed instantly. The alleys were narrow, and the buildings were three or four stories high. You could see very little once down in the alleyways, save the slippery stone path ahead and a few adjacent buildings, which were all painted in shades of yellow and beige. It was cooler as the direct sun could not reach the alleys. It was also much quieter as the alleys in the *medina* are too narrow for cars and this part of the *medina* was not crowded. We made our way through the maze. A right here, a left there, then a right and another right. It was soon evident that we had entered another world - mysterious, captivating, and timeless. My emotions raced back and forth between exhilaration and claustrophobia. In a quarter mile of walking a dozen centuries had disappeared beneath our feet.

After a bit we could hear a mesmerizing chant as though coming from an echo chamber. When we approached the source of the chanting, we saw an elderly blind beggar in a brown *djellaba* sitting cross legged in a corner that had been clearly chosen for its splendid acoustic qualities. His chanting of the *Qur'an* resonated off the walls and hung in the air like incense for the ears. It was so enchanting that I instinctively gave him some money.

Momi said, "You know my friend, I think he now has more money than you."

It was an appropriate reminder of my new station in life that quickly brought me back to earth. As we continued, the alleys became more crowded, as little shops were opening for the evening. At this location, there were shops with varieties of dates, nuts, and spices in cone shaped piles. It was refreshing to see food displayed in the open, in bulk, and without plastic packaging. Most of the shops were colorful and artfully detailed. In fact, they were more than shops; they were galleries, and the proud smiles of the shopkeepers told you that they agreed.

As we continued, we passed bazaars with attractive carpets and kilims draped outside. There were shops with men sitting out front pressing gold leaf designs onto handmade leather products. We heard the musical clatter of men and boys hammering out intricate Islamic designs on brass and copper lamps, bowls, kettles, trays, candlesticks, and pots. Other men were cutting out designs in brass lanterns that were like metal lace. There were potters ever so carefully painting intricate blue designs on pieces as small as ashtrays and as large as three-foot-high urns. Still other shops created wood trunks with multi-colored Islamic designs. Finally, we came upon the craftsman chipping Morocco's world-renowned *zellije* mosaic tile work. As an artist myself, I was thoroughly humbled by a city that worked tirelessly to create amazing handcrafts with patience and precision.

We arrived at the famous Karaouine Mosque with its graceful arches, exquisitely carved Islamic designs, and green tiled roofs. I instantly recognized it as the place in the poster we had seen in the Gibraltar travel agency window which had attracted us into coming to Morocco. It is the most visible structure in the *medina* and is said to accommodate 20,000 worshippers. It is also home to the world's oldest university, which was established in 857 A.D. by a wealthy woman who had migrated to Fez from Kairouan, Tunisia. There was a small fountain with men washing themselves before entering. I would later learn that we were not the only ones attracted to the Karaouine. Centuries earlier it had been the guiding light and magnet for scholars from around the world at a time when Europe had fallen into the Dark Ages. It is why Fez is said to be the religious and intellectual capital of Morocco.

We passed a long row of textile and candle shops that finally led up the street to a fabulous shrine. Momi explained, "This is the Moulay Idriss

II *zawiya* (tomb). Moulay Idriss is the founder and patron saint of Fez. This is a very holy place; you are fortunate to have come here."

In many respects Fez was exceeding my expectations. I saw some incredible architecture that spoke to my heart and raised my spirits, yet I also sensed it was from another era, when this city had been more prosperous, more spiritually uplifted. Efforts had begun to restore her treasures, but they took a long time to build, and they would take a long time to resurrect.

Aside from our brief transit in Tangier and a childhood excursion into Tijuana, Mexico, this was my first visit to the so-called "Third World." I would eventually adjust my sensitivities, but my first walk through the *medina* was also fairly shocking. My nose was on a roller coaster ride, at one moment exhilarated by the stacks of fresh mint lining the street, the next moment suffocating from the stench from a wall turned into a urinal or worse. Beggars were everywhere and children were clawing at us for a few pennies. I would later learn that some of it was well rehearsed theater to make money off the tourists, yet there was also genuine poverty. Perhaps most disconcerting of all were the insults hurled at us by young men who seemed to feel obliged to challenge every tourist.

In retrospect, I am reminded of the movie based on Paul Bowles' book *Sheltering Skies*. Morocco tugs at one's senses in two directions. It is simultaneously one of the most beautiful places you have ever seen, as well as one of the most wretched places you have ever been. The challenge for the visitor is to learn how to keep the latter in check.

The next morning, we went to the American Cultural Center to report our lost passports and get information on getting some money sent from home. The Center was run by a young Foreign Service Officer by the name of Chris Ross. He was friendly, comforting, and clearly a very sharp guy. Years later, he would become the American Ambassador in Algeria and later in Syria. He was widely respected for his command of Arabic and skills of diplomacy, and it was our good fortune to stumble into his office.

As it turned out, the thief had thrown my wallet with our passports and everything else except our money into a mailbox. I was to learn that Moroccan thieves do have a heart. In New York, they might kill you for your watch. In Morocco, at least in those days, they only wanted your money; they didn't violate you beyond that. Mr. Ross loaned us some money out of his own pocket and arranged for the Embassy to receive money from our parents and let us make collect calls home.

I woke my dad in the middle of the night in Oregon. He was glad to hear my voice as I had been living overseas for a year, and I rarely called home on account of the exorbitant expense of overseas calls in those days. I told him I was fine but in a jam. I was in Morocco and had been robbed.

"Morocco" he repeated, "I don't know, isn't that a little rich for our blood, and you know how I feel about gambling."

"Dad, I didn't say Monaco, I said Morocco - as in the movie Casablanca."

There was silence at the other end.

"Dad, you still there?"

"Yeah, but the more I hear, the worse this sounds."

I told my dad I loved him and promised to be careful.

As I hung up and turned around, Mary Ann was laughing.

"Monaco?" she asked.

"Yeah," I said, "Princess Grace and I have been having this thing. I wasn't going to tell you, but I guess I have to now."

A couple of days later we went by the Cultural Center to see if our money had come in. Thank God it had. While we were signing some release forms, I asked Mr. Ross if there were other Americans besides him who lived in Fez. He said, "Not many. Five Peace Corpsmen, one USAID guy, and five English teachers here at our Language Center."

Then his eyes lit up. "Are you interested in teaching English?"

We replied that neither of us had training in teaching English as a foreign language. He explained that it wasn't required.

"Given what little we pay, we can't require any certificates. We just need people with some intelligence who speak clearly. You seem to qualify. Do you have any other skills?"

I showed him some sketches that I had done on the trip, and I explained that I had done a little graphic design back in the States. His eyes lit up again,

"As a matter of fact, we need someone to design posters to publicize the English program and take care of our window displays. I am in the process of setting up a program to teach English through the Arts. It is called the *Melting Pot Club*. We already have a couple who do a folk music program that has been wildly popular. Robbie and Honey from New York have a weekly session with a hundred students who can sing Bob Dylan tunes by heart."

Mary Ann explained that she had nearly completed her degree in public relations and writing, so a deal was struck. Mary Ann would teach a class in creative writing, and I would teach an art class. After a few months, we would create a magazine with the students' work. In the evenings we would teach at the American Language Center. We were ecstatic at how quickly our fortunes had turned. It seemed that fate wanted us to learn more about this intriguing place.

We returned to Momi's, now more relaxed knowing that we had respectable jobs and our days at his pipe factory were numbered. However, that evening Momi rushed in clearly in a panic. His father was returning sooner than expected. Our next surprise turned out to be that his father was a policeman with two families. He had been staying with family number two and now he was coming back to be with family number one; the pipe factory was closing until further notice.

We moved to a hotel and started making plans for our new careers. A few days later we began to look for an apartment with Momi's help. As we toured around, Momi began to fill us in on some of the other complexities in his young life. He had planned to marry a young woman by the name of Kinza but there were problems over the dowry, furniture, and such, so now their respective parents were at loggerheads.

We learned that in Morocco, marriages were often arranged. A big part of the problem was that Momi found the young lady without the assistance of his parents, upsetting the social fabric. Kinza's parents had nominally accepted the marriage, but they kept throwing up roadblocks.

We naively consented to allow them to stay in the extra bedroom in the apartment we rented until they could work things out. Momi had rescued us, now it was our turn to help him. What we didn't realize is what a hornet's nest we had stepped in.

Of course, that was 1971 and Morocco has changed a great deal since then. Nonetheless many of the events chronicled in this book are about Moroccan mysticism. They are true accounts which demonstrate the elasticity of time and space, which is to say they are timeless. They are as relevant today as they were then or will be in a hundred years.

Karaouine Mosque - Fez

Moulay Idriss Mausoleum - Fez

Fez carpet bazaar

Embroidery supplies - Fez

3 - WORKING AT THE CULTURAL CENTER

Classes were scheduled to start soon, so we were sent to Rabat for a two-week seminar on Teaching English as a Foreign Language (TEFL) Most TEFL instructors have master's degrees in the subject from a proper university. We on the other hand were taking a two-week cram course. Rabat is the modern-day capital of Morocco and is on the Atlantic coastline an hour and a half north of Casablanca. One of the first things that I noticed in Rabat was that the old walls that once surrounded the city looked like they had been shot up leaving pock marks all over. I asked the seminar leader which period of history the holes came from, and I got a strange look.

"Are you joking or haven't you seen a newspaper lately?"

I confessed that I hadn't read a newspaper or watched television for several months.

"My advice is that you start reading newspapers when you travel. There was a *coup* attempt a few days ago. The King was nearly killed, and several foreign ambassadors were killed. Things are still pretty shaky".

I resolved to keep a closer watch on the news in future and it was a good thing. My stay in Morocco turned out to be one of its more turbulent chapters in the country's long and colorful history. There would be at least two more *coup* attempts, and a major confrontation with Spain while I was there.

As for Rabat, it is a pleasant city, although lacking in the historical and architectural wonders found in Fez. Due to its location on the coast the weather is mild. There are unspoiled beaches to the north and south. Its *kasbah* is small but clean and easy to negotiate. The embassies had given rise to several fine international restaurants and the Rabatis had it pretty good when the bullets weren't flying.

Our two weeks passed pleasantly despite the locals' jagged nerves. I felt more comfortable in Rabat in the aftermath of the *coup* attempt than I did in Tangier on a sleepy afternoon. We had a pleasant room in a French era hotel in the new city. It had an attractive tile floor and a lovely garden where we breakfasted daily on *café au lait* and *croissants*. I was beginning to settle into the Moroccan/French lifestyle.

After our return to Fez, I made a strategic decision to hole up in the apartment until I could speak some Arabic. I felt too vulnerable to the young hustlers and was generally suffering from the crossed wires of miscommunication. In those days, English was not widely spoken outside of hotels and tourist shops. The little French that I studied in high school was not serving me particularly well. One day I was having a hard time getting a taxi driver to understand my mispronunciation of the French word *rue*. After much frustration he finally caught on. Then he used his hands to show me that the Arabic word for street is *shari'* which I repeated without hesitation.

Then my driver clapped and laughed loudly, and shouted, "*al-hamdullah* (praise be to God), you Arab, no *Francais*." I got his point and asked one of the Arabic speaking English teachers for help. Her name was Kinza. (She is not the same Kinza mentioned earlier.) Sometimes Moroccans would assign Americans Moroccan names if they couldn't pronounce or remember their name. Kinza was the director of the language center and had come to Morocco several years prior with the Peace Corps. She supplied me with some transliterated Arabic study guides (using Latin letters to phonetically spell Arabic words) and got me started using the Peace Corps system of drilling basic vocabulary without any reference to English. Kinza's husband Phil was a musicologist who researched and recorded Moroccan traditional music. Phil and Kinza were deeply immersed in Moroccan culture and set a good example for the rest of us to get past our own cultural comfort zones.

One of the great things about speaking Arabic as a foreigner was that even attempting a little of it was received warmly and opened doors that might otherwise remain closed. Arabs were not used to Westerners making the effort to learn their language and there was the implicit suggestion that you respected their culture and were willing to meet them on their terms. I can't tell you how many times I heard Moroccans express wonder at how much Arabic I was speaking in a short period, as compared to Frenchmen who had lived there for twenty years and still didn't know more than a few words.

Sometimes their amazement at my feeble attempts at Arabic gave me pause for thought. Many of them spoke three or more languages, why was it so surprising that an American could speak a little of their language? Did they think we were all stupid or linguistically impaired? Of course, most Americans are linguistically impaired. We don't emphasize foreign languages partly because we can travel thousands of miles across our country without need to speak another language.

Then there is the matter that English is the international language. Everyone is expected to learn English. Some Moroccans even suggested that I was foolish to learn their language which I didn't really require. Of course, this is part of the reason Americans have a hard time learning languages. Everyone wants to practice their English and we lack opportunities (and consequently the necessity) to speak the other languages.

However, I was very fortunate in this respect. Robby and Honey had a Moroccan friend who heard that I was studying Arabic and he invited me to his home. His name was Abdesalam Ketami. Abdesalam was a prince among men, and this book is dedicated to him.

Abdesalam was a short round man with a round always-beaming face accented by one gold tooth. He came from Chaouen, an idyllic town located 130 miles north of Fez in the Rif Mountains. He was married to a rather tall woman from the same town, and they were without children. This is generally a difficult thing for Arabs and would normally lead to divorce. But Abdesalam and Rochma were a happy couple and Abdesalam would never consider abandoning a friend. He had his own sense of honor and wasn't too concerned with the preoccupations of others.

Perhaps it was because they had no children that he became a grade schoolteacher. He had a special gift for teaching and sensing the minds of children. At the end of each day, he would have his students sit quietly on top of their desks and watch the sunlight move about the room.

I once brought him a gift of a large block of Gouda cheese wrapped in red cellophane to his summer home on the Mediterranean. He was thrilled, but not with the cheese. He took the red cellophane and made sunglasses for the children of his poor fisherman neighbor. I'll never forget the joy on the faces of these kids running about in their red sunglasses.

During the school year, Abdesalam and Rochma lived in a small apartment in the part of Fez called *fesjdeed* (New Fez in Arabic although it hadn't been new since the 13th century.) Their apartment was small, but had a very pleasant roof-top garden, which was a real blessing in those days before air conditioning. They grew plants in recycled powdered milk cans and had a lush garden. I spent many wonderful hours seated on a carpet and pillows in that garden getting Arabic lessons, listening to the alley below, and learning about Moroccan culture.

Abdesalam spent most of his time out on his rooftop garden reading the *Qur'an* or the Bible, as well as studying German (he already spoke Arabic, French, Spanish & English.) He learned English at an early age from missionary nuns in his hometown, which at that time was under

Spanish occupation. The nuns used the Bible as his English primer and he consequently spoke Old English. You can imagine the surprise of the first English-speaking tourists who happened upon Chaouen and were greeted by this smiling child.

"Hark, dear friends, doest thou knoweth thy way through our merry town?"

It didn't take long before we concluded that we had paid off our hospitality debt to Momi and started looking for a single bedroom apartment. We quickly found a modern apartment in the *Ville Nouvelle*. It was centrally located and not far from the Center. It was just a couple of blocks from a small grocery store as well as a fruit and vegetable shop. The owner of the vegetable shop was tickled that I was learning Arabic, so he insisted that before I could order I had to repeat after him the name of every fruit and vegetable that he neatly stacked in cone shaped piles on stands. This added a fair amount of time to my shopping, but the other shoppers didn't mind. In fact, listening to me mispronounce the names of the vegetables became the most popular comedy show in town.

One night we had Rochma and Abdesalam to dinner. After I cleared the plates from the table, Abdesalam told us that we really needed to get a maid. I wasn't quite sure he was serious.

"You know, Abdesalam, we are far too poor to even consider having a maid, and anyway I was raised working class. My dad would have a heart attack if he heard I had a maid."

Abdesalam laughed and explained that he understood that we didn't earn much by American standards, but by Moroccans standards it was something different all together.

Abdesalam went on, "In Morocco we believe that people who can afford it have a social responsibility to hire a maid. It is a way to spread wealth and everyone benefits. Having a job not only helps the maid's family, but it gives her a sense of dignity. That is especially true if she is working for foreigners because it is known that they pay more, and presumably get the most qualified maids."

Abdesalam said that he knew a neighbor lady who badly needed some extra income. If we had her come just one day a week and paid her twenty dollars, she would be thrilled to cook and clean."

We agreed and the arrangement mostly worked out very well. She made delicious Moroccan dishes and was a good baker. There was just one thing, she refused to use hot water to clean the dishes or laundry because *djinn* (spirits) live in the plumbing and it would be VERY bad to scald them.

At first, we didn't know what to do, then we concluded our germ exposure in Morocco was already so high, a few more wouldn't make much difference. It was just one more oddity in our life in Morocco. We didn't have a car, but we had a maid.

Our work at the Center had settled in with one notable exception. Along with teaching English and art classes, I had been assigned to design the display windows that ran along the boulevard. The Center was at the end of the boulevard that led to the *medina* and consequently there was a lot of foot traffic past our display windows. Chris had become frustrated with the normal USIS (US Information Service) approach, which was frankly transparent propaganda. He felt he had been making more headway at improving Moroccan attitudes toward the U.S. by emphasizing cultural themes and playing down our policies, which were usually at odds with the Arab World. Chris asked me to bring some creativity to the window displays, perhaps draw attention to the art classes.

I decided to do something in the way of 'pop art.' While I wasn't really a big fan of Andy Warhol, I concluded that the Campbell soup can approach might be more interesting if you had never seen a can of Campbell soup. At that time, very few consumer products were being imported to Morocco from the U.S. and I thought it might be interesting to work some commercial packaging into a 'concept art' display.

Chris and his wife Carol did much of their shopping at the PX at the U.S. airbase at Kenitra, so I explained to Carol my plan. She generously gave me access to her pantry. I helped myself to a little of this and that and put it all in a clear garbage bag. I then mounted the bag on a board in one of the Center's display windows. I added an explanation about 'concept art' being a modern art movement and how that which is one person's trash might be another person's art. Then I headed upstairs to the office.

I had not been upstairs very long before I started hearing some commotion down on the street. Chris and I stepped out onto the balcony. More and more people were gathering. I was momentarily pleased with the great reaction my art display seemed to be getting. But Chris burst my balloon my telling me that they were yelling "Americans go home" and "death to infidels."

"You better have some answers before I throw you to them," Chris said with a certain amount of sincerity.

I said there were just soup cans, instant cake mix boxes, cereal boxes and a loaf of sliced bread.

"Oh my God," he exclaimed, running down the stairs. He talked to the crowd, then let himself into the display window, pulled out the sliced bread, stuck it up on a ledge, and again begged for the crowd's forgiveness. Apparently satisfied, the crowd began to disperse. I don't like white bread myself but was bewildered and amazed by what I had just witnessed.

Chris returned flustered but chuckling, "I suppose you don't have a clue as to what you just did, do you?"

"Not really."

"Bread is a holy sacrament to the Moroccans. They never throw it away. Start looking around, you'll see bread on ledges and window seals, but never in the trash. You, my friend, not only stuck bread in the trash but put it in a display window which they interpreted as an act of disrespect and defiance from the American government. From now on, you'd better show me any displays before they go in the window. Other than that, your display was interesting. Just be careful. You are a fish out of water. Make an effort to know what offends your new neighbors."

Despite this misstep, work continued to go very well. The students were friendly, eager, and easy to work with. In fact, in some respects things were going too well. There weren't many options for students in Fez and consequently we were swamped. Then there were some student protests and we suddenly found ourselves in the company of those opposed to the government, which was definitely not the policy of the State Department. In time, word would come down that we had to distance ourselves from the students. But while it lasted it was very refreshing to be around their bubbling creativity and energy. I sensed that Morocco had a bright future if this generation was given the opportunity to follow their dreams.

Most of these young folks were quite poor. I once invited a few of them to a French style restaurant in the *Ville Nouvelle* near the Center. One of them declined and I persisted in making sure that he understood that I was paying. He still declined even though I knew that he wanted to be with the group. I asked him what the deal was.

"I've never been to a Western restaurant, I wouldn't know what to do," he explained shyly.

I was fairly shocked that this otherwise urbane eighteen-year-old had never been in any of the many French style restaurants that lined the boulevards of the *Ville Nouvelle*.

"Look, Ali, you speak English better than most Americans, I think you are destined to see the world, you are going to have to learn about Western restaurants sooner or later. Believe me, these people should be honored to have you in their restaurant."

After lunch, I asked Ali, how his meal was.

"Thank you for your generosity Mr. Bill, but you know I could have fed my family for a month on what you spent for our meal," he said sincerely.

I suppose this shouldn't have come as such a surprise to me even though it wasn't a particularly expensive restaurant. I realized that I had a lot to learn from the students - the conditions in which they were raised, their character, and their dedication to their studies, for their own futures, as well as those of their extended families.

Ali later won a scholarship for summer study in London. After his return, we asked him what were the most interesting things he saw in London.

Ali replied with his eyes wide open in amazement, "Many of the older women had blue hair, the milkmen delivered milk early in the morning and just left it in front of the stores, and nobody stole it. When I went to the bus terminal everyone was standing in line and there wasn't any pushing." (What strange people, these Brits!)

Another student named Ahmed invited us to his home for lunch. His mother was widowed, and the family was living in very modest, yet proud circumstances. They put on a delightful feast for us that humbled us by the trouble to which they had gone. I have kept in touch with Ahmed over the years. He became wealthy in Morocco's construction boom and is now retired. He has kept me plugged into Morocco by sending videos of family weddings, his travels around the country, and Moroccan music. Ahmed gave me a valuable lesson in how much you can immerse yourself in a culture by digital time travel – a case of the student becoming the teacher's teacher.

At work we developed a close relationship with the secretary, Naima Belghiti. Naima began working at the Center right out of high school and had been there for fifteen years. Her husband was an up-and-coming police officer, and she was the 'can do' person for the Center. Besides taking care of the Center's needs, she also looked after the American staff, directing them where to buy their necessities and clueing them in about Moroccan customs and traditions. She was indispensable.

As my own familiarity with Fez and Arabic grew, Chris started asking me to help in showing around visiting American dignitaries and journalists. One such person was the U.S. District Attorney of New Jersey. He asked us to keep the nature of his visit quiet because back home he was prosecuting the very high profile "French Connection."

He came to Fez at the request of his wife's family. His young brother-in-law had been arrested with a kilo of hashish at a roadblock between Fez and Ketama. Ketama is Morocco's hashish producing region. At least in those days, hashish cultivation was a relatively innocent tribal tradition.

We frequently got calls from the prison saying that they had some American incarcerated with the locals. The last thing the Moroccans wanted to do was to house and feed young Americans. But it was a good opportunity to raise a little cash - the Moroccan equivalent of a speed trap. Morocco had a reputation as being a place where hashish is cheap and readily available but there were a lot of double standards and gray areas at play. One of the complications was that although possession of hashish by itself was a minor offense, Moroccans often mixed it with tobacco and failure to pay the tobacco tax was a major offense. Furthermore, the *Regie de Tabacs* had a habit of prosecuting foreigners for violation of the tax law regardless of whether their hash was mixed with tobacco or not.

When I took the DA over to the prison, he noticed that there were lots of Moroccan men leaning up against the outside prison walls smoking hash or *keef* (*keef* is the flower of the cannabis plant). He was incredulous that these Moroccans were openly smoking in front of the prison and there were Americans locked up inside for doing the same thing.

I had to explain to him that it wasn't exactly the same. His brother-in-law had a larger quantity and being a foreigner, one might easily surmise that he planned to get into an export business that was reserved for Moroccans. The other factor is that you can't fine the Moroccan guys who were leaning against the wall, because they didn't have any money. The DA was catching on, but his American legal background was impeding him from having a complete grasp.

After a couple of weeks, the DA's brother-in-law was called before a judge. As I predicted, the judge quickly fined him the equivalent of $1700. Against my advice, the DA stood up and asked to address the court. He asked me to tell the judge that he was family of the defendant and the judge agreed to hear him. So, the DA insisted that I explain who he was and that this young man came from an influential family in the U.S., and they hoped to be treated with appropriate deference. I tried to tell him that was not a good idea as fines were typically assessed according to family's ability to pay and the judge might perceive his request as disrespectful. However, the DA persisted.

The judge recessed momentarily to consider this important revelation. He came back and announced that the fine was now $3400. The DA jumped up to protest, but I grabbed his arm and whispered to him, "Unless you are carrying $6800, I would sit down." He paused, sat down, then arranged to pay $3400 for his lesson in Moroccan law.

After several visits to the prisons, I became curious about this place Ketama. I had heard how beautiful it was and indeed these were the green Rif Mountains that I had seen while sailing into Gibraltar on the trimaran. So, one weekend I slipped on my long, dark blue hooded *djellaba* that made me relatively indiscernible from a Moroccan - at least as long as I sauntered with the appropriate gait that Abdesalam so carefully taught me.

The road from Fez to Ketama starts by ambling through gently rolling olive tree covered hills for a couple of hours until the road steepens, and pine and fir trees take over. The road hugs high cliffs that fall rather sharply down to a river. Terraces are carved out below and one can see the crops. From high up on the road, you might assume that they were growing corn or wheat. But arable land is scarce, and one suspects that as much of the land as possible is dedicated to a much more profitable crop.

I stayed a night at the Ketama Hotel and spoke to no one besides the desk clerk and a couple of waiters. I said very little as I didn't want to tip my hand that I was not Moroccan. I sat in the lobby with my *djellaba* hood covering my blonde hair, pretending to read an Arabic newspaper. At some couches nearby, a young American guy was not too quietly conducting negotiations for a hash deal. The Moroccan who was making the deal eventually got up and went over to a man that I determined was a plain clothes policeman (in this case a plain *djellaba*). In Arabic, he told him the American would have the stuff and was leaving for Fez on the morning bus - the same one I would take.

I got a good night's rest in the clear mountain air, had a light breakfast of Moroccan bread, olives, almonds, and Turkish coffee. Then I headed over to the small bus station, as the bus left early for the several-hour trip to Fez. When I boarded the bus, it was already packed with forty villagers, the young American with his brick of hash, the undercover cop, and a couple dozen chickens. It was another pretty drive through the mountains. The locals had lived in semi-autonomy for hundreds of years. The Moroccan sultans had long ago learned to leave these fearless mountain people alone. The Spanish ruled northern Morocco for a period before 1956 but they too never really controlled these mountains. I admired the Rifis (residents of the Rif Mountains). Coming from the mountainous western state of Oregon, I could relate to these stubborn mountain people.

The young American was seated near the front of the bus. I was in the middle, and the policeman stayed in the back watching his prey. I was also watching the young American, knowing more or less what kind of fate lay ahead for him, which is to say nothing too awful. After all, this wasn't Turkey and he wasn't going to waste his young life away in a squalid prison for his bad judgment, as did the young man in the movie *Midnight Express*. A couple of weeks in jail and $1700 of his parents' hard-earned cash and he would be on his way. I thought about my own parents and how they too often had picked up the tab for my poor choices.

I also thought about the stories that some of the Americans coming out of the prison told me about Moroccan prisoners being tortured in front of them, just to play with their suburban heads. I started to sympathize with my countryman who was on the verge of a similar experience. Americans in Morocco tended to stick together whether they had anything in common or not. When you are overseas you are generally less judgmental of your American comrades. You know that your survival might one day depend upon them. I thought about the guys in Viet Nam depending on their buddies. Did they really care whether another guy bought some hash once?

Then I tried to look at it from the other side. People are trying to keep their kids away from drugs and this guy is trying to smuggle drugs just to make some money. He made his bed; he will have to sleep in it. I continued to wrestle with the idea of tipping him off but couldn't quite bring myself to do it.

About halfway to Fez, the bus pulled over for a little pit stop for at a roadside cafe. I ordered some brochettes and a coke and sat down at the last vacant table. Pretty soon the American came over. He was all nervous smiles and sat down. "You speak English?"

I nodded, barely looking up. I was uncomfortable with being associated with someone who was in hot, hot water.

"Wow what a terrific place. This has been the trip of a lifetime. It'll take me a couple of years to pay my dad back, but it's been worth every penny."

That pretty well tipped the scales for me. I pulled my hood back a bit, revealing some of my blonde hair and whispered, "You are not in Disneyland here you know. There is a cop on the bus who has been with you ever since the hotel. You better get smart before it is too late." I went back to my sandwich.

He got up, not sure if I was just messing with him or what. He went back to the counter and looked around as he ordered more food. Then he saw the cop looking at him. He clearly realized it was the guy who had been in the hotel. He put his head down and got back on the bus.

I was somewhat surprised that there wasn't a roadblock set up outside of Fez. I concluded that was probably because it was just one guy on a bus and the cop on the bus was sufficient. He would follow him to the terminal, slap handcuffs on him and drag him off to the prison.

However, as we approached the first gate to the Fez *medina*, a young couple with three small children stood up and started moving to the front of the bus, even though the bus had not yet come to a stop. When the bus finally stopped, I noticed that the American's seat was empty and so did the cop. I looked out the window and the American was scampering toward the gate to the *medina*. The cop jumped up but was slowed by the couple who were getting their kids down from the bus. Before the cop could pull up his *djellaba* and give chase, the guy had already disappeared into the *medina*.

The maze of alleys that made up the *medina* may have worked for or against the American, but more than likely it made the cop's job of finding him extremely difficult. The people on the street probably wouldn't have helped the cop, even to chase down an American. This one probably got away.

I reflected upon my role in this little soap opera. My sense of nationalism had completely taken over. I thought about the Moroccans at the train station in Tangier blocking me as I tried to run after the guy who stole my wallet. It seemed that they had this one coming. In any case, I had become as fatalistic as the Moroccans. I wouldn't lose any sleep, one way or the other. Whatever was God's will was fine with me. At least I made it a sporting event. I was satisfied with that.

There were other cases that were more complicated. We once received a call that an American was being held in the psychiatric hospital. Chris was getting fed up with going to the prison - and now they were referring psychiatric cases. His primary mission at the cultural center was to schmooze Moroccan officials, not to work out the problems of American hippies. Consequently, Chris asked Mary Ann and I to go to the nut house and check out what this guy's condition was and determine whether he should really be there.

We arranged to meet the guy. He seemed a little spacy, but that wasn't particularly uncommon for the hippie tourists coming through Fez. He said he thought he was being persecuted for political reasons. I asked what kind of politics he was involved in. He said he wasn't personally involved in anything. It was for what he had seen. He said he had been on *Avenue Borj Nord*, and a black limo and several cars came racing by, there was some gunfire, and he took cover.

"Actually I didn't see that much. I was just trying to get out of the way. A little while later the police nabbed me and brought me here. I'm not crazy, they just think I might know something that I shouldn't."

It sounded like classic schizophrenia except for the fact that we also had heard rumors that there was another *coup* attempt while the King was in town. Had he heard the same rumors and just fabricated this into a defense of why he shouldn't be locked up? We weren't really convinced one way or the other. He certainly wasn't noticeably out of touch. He claimed that he had been given shock treatment several times. If true, that might have explained some of his spaciness.

We reported to Chris that it was hard to get a clear picture of the guy's mental state. So, Chris said that he would try to check out the rumors about the *coup* attempt. In the meantime, there wasn't much he could do.

It wasn't another two weeks before we heard about another American showing up at the psychiatric hospital. For a couple of days, we thought it was just another report about the guy we had talked to. However, it was indeed a second case. This time the guy was nabbed going house to house in the *medina*, nude and asking to use people's phones. In Morocco that kind of behavior certainly qualifies as crazy. In those days, wearing shorts could get you in big trouble and you definitely had to be nuts to think you could find a phone in the *medina*.

So, we were off to the funny farm again. This time they wouldn't let us see the patient but gave us an appointment with the French psychiatrist in charge of the hospital. The minute we met the psychiatrist chills went down our spines. He hadn't brushed his teeth or changed his shirt in a month and his office was crammed full of very ordinary rocks. He laughed at his own bad jokes with such vigor that he could hardly bring himself under control. We got out of there ASAP.

Chris was somewhat skeptical of our description of the good doctor, but he called the hospital and got more information on the patient and had the State Department track down his parents. They arrived two days later, exhausted from their flight from California but we took them straight to the hospital where they demanded to see their son. We were not allowed to go in with them. They returned five minutes later, the mother sobbing and the father shaking.

"What kind of hospital is this? He is unconscious and lying in an Asian toilet and he's got crap in his hair. I can't believe this?" the mother cried in disbelief.

We assured them that we would do everything possible to get him out right away. We returned to the Center and told Chris what was going on and he left directly for the hospital and insisted on a meeting with the psychiatrist. It took Chris but one look to know that that this physician was not well. Yet, he treated him very professionally. Chris asked about the accuracy of the parents' description of their son's condition. The doctor laughed uncontrollably for a moment and then responded, "You know if we treat them too nicely, they wouldn't want to leave, would they?"

I had always respected Chris, but it wasn't until that moment that I realized what a truly powerful force he was. He looked the doctor sternly in the eye and in a calm forceful voice said, "Doctor, that is not an acceptable medical practice in your homeland and certainly not in mine. You WILL release the two American patients into my custody tomorrow at 8:00 a.m. They will be showered, shaved and in clean clothes. Do we understand each other?"

The doctor fidgeted nervously, "But you are not a doctor, how can you take responsibility for these patients?"

"These men are American citizens, and I am a Foreign Service Officer of the United States of America. It is my responsibility to see that these men get proper medical care. I will see you at 8 o'clock."

"Well, if you insist," the doctor complained.

"I insist," Chris calmly countered.

That next morning, we picked up the two shaved, showered, and cleanly clothed men, and along with the two parents, delivered them to the American Embassy in Rabat. A consular officer checked them into Rabat's relatively modern hospital where they stayed for several days before returning to the States.

Several months later we received a package from the former streaker. It contained tapes recorded from a California radio station. A letter explained that he hoped the tapes would make us feel closer to home. He said he was working again and had gotten his life together. He thanked us for helping to get him out of his crisis. It made us feel good, but of course I knew that it was really Chris Ross who had stepped up to the plate.

The next confirmed *coup* attempt against the King was quite spectacular. The King was returning from Europe with many of his ministers. Suddenly four Moroccan fighter jets appeared and began shooting the plane to pieces. Many of the ministers were killed and the King narrowly escaped death. The plane began to lose control. Being a pilot himself, the King reportedly rushed to the cockpit and assumed the reins from the dead pilot .

The King then got on the plane's radio and said to one of the pilots of the attacking planes, "This is the co-pilot, you have killed the King, the pilot and many ministers are dead. I am just a professional military pilot like you. You accomplished your mission, let me see my children tonight." The plane was allowed to land.

Once on the ground, a small black Fiat was waiting for the King. He got in and raced off to a hidden location. For days the country thought the King had been killed. We heard rumors of celebrations in the streets of some cities and villages. Without a doubt the King's popularity was at an all-time low at that time, and there were many who would have been happy to see him gone. We heard stories of people in some cities prematurely dancing in the streets, for which they allegedly paid a high price.

However, the King was like a cat who had nine lives. Moroccans call it *baraka*, which literally means blessed, although it can also refer to certain magical force. Some skeptics believed that Hassan II fabricated these *coup* attempts in order enhance this image of *baraka*. I personally think that is quite unlikely. I have heard and read too many credible sources verifying the accounts. In fact, at first the Moroccans thought that the CIA was behind the *coup* attempt. In the aftermath of the assault American personnel at the airbase in Kenitra had Moroccan tanks pointing at the windows of their residences until the crisis had passed.

My sister Kathryn Gray, her husband Steve and children Kelly, Kami, Jeff, and Shan also got waylaid in the scary episode. They had been living in Morocco for a number of months as part of their European-Moroccan sabbatical adventure. (Kelly and Kami, aged eight and six were the only ones among us who showed any real aptitude for Arabic.) However, as they were returning to Europe, they were driving to Tangier to catch a ferry. As they neared Kenitra all hell was breaking loose, and they got snared in a very tense military roadblock.

Kenitra is the home of Morocco's largest airbase, which is co-located with the U.S.'s only Moroccan military base. The four F-5 fighter jets that had just attacked the King's plane had flown out of Kenitra. All four pilots had been trained in the U.S. and were friendly with U.S. personnel at Kenitra. Consequently, paranoia about possible U.S. involvement was understandable.

Not surprisingly, the soldiers at the roadblock found it highly suspicious that the Gray family just happened along at this inauspicious moment in Moroccan history, so they pulled the Grays over for interrogation.

Naturally the first thing the interrogators wanted to know was whether Steve was a current or former member of the U.S. military. Steve reluctantly acknowledged that he had been an officer and pilot in the Air Force. Strike one! And oh, by the way, why have you kidnapped that Moroccan child in the back seat? Strike two!

At this point Kathryn jumped in. Pretty much everywhere they went in Morocco there were scenes, as Moroccans assumed that the Grays' two-year-old Shan was a kidnapped Moroccan. That is because Shan was adopted and he is African American. Kathryn anticipated there could issues, so before leaving the U.S. she had the kids put on her passport.

The interrogator carefully inspected Kathryn's passport and that resolved the kidnapping charge, but Steve's status was still in limbo. Fortunately, Kathryn was an attractive thirty-year-old blonde who was fluent in French. She was able to hold the interrogator's attention long enough to convince him that the only thing the Grays were in danger of was missing their ferry.

The other weird connection to the *coup* attempt was that the pilot of one of the attacking jets was from Chaouen and the boyhood friend of my friend Abdelsalam. Abdesalam was naturally saddened by the death of his friend, who had been quickly executed. I was not completely sure of how Abdesalam felt about the King. He was certainly very patriotic but had never really said anything one way or the other about the King. However, I was trying to get a sense whether Abdesalam saw his pilot friend as a martyr or a disgrace. Abdesalam considered the question carefully, "You know, I do not envy His Majesty. A king has many grave responsibilities. Consequently, he has many opportunities to make mistakes and unlike you and I, his mistakes will affect millions of people. No, I don't envy His Majesty, his road to Glory will necessarily be long and bumpy.

King Mohammed V Mausoleum - Rabat

Center Staff Bottom: Amb. Chris Ross & Carol, Tony, Abdelkrim Ouazzani, Naima Belghiti, Tamu. Top: Ameur Tazi, Abdeslam, Mohammed Alami, Kaddour el-Mrini, Ahmed Bennis, Layashi Filali.

Abdesalam's wife Rochma

Ketama – Rif Mountains

Women working the cannabis fields

Our housekeeper Tahara

4 - ON THE ROAD AGAIN

During the 1972 summer break we decided that we should buy a camping van. We had been in Morocco for a year without a car and we were getting restless to see more of the countryside, and public transportation was limited. I made the trip up to Ketama on the bus and we took the train to Rabat but there was so much more to see. We also wanted to go places where there weren't hotels. Abdesalam and Rochma had invited us to stay with them at their house on the Mediterranean, southeast of Tangier, but their place was quite small, and we would have to camp on the beach. We decided that what we really needed was a used VW van.

In those days, most Moroccans didn't have vehicles as they were prohibitively expensive because of a 100% import tax. We had heard that Volkswagens were dirt cheap in Amsterdam. If we had Netherlands plates on the car, we would have to leave Morocco every six months to avoid the import tax but that wasn't a major problem. As foreigners all we had to do was drive across the border at either Ceuta or Melilla - the two Spanish enclaves on the Moroccan Mediterranean coast.

So, we flew to Amsterdam and spent a few days seeing the city, shopping for a van, then getting the newly purchased van ready for camping. We camped our way south through France, down the Spanish Mediterranean coast, took a ferry across the Strait of Gibraltar from Algeciras, Spain, and landed at the Spanish enclave Ceuta. From there we drove another hour and a half south to Abdesalam and Rochma's home in Oued Laou, which fifty years ago was just a sleepy little fishing village.

Oued means river or valley in Arabic. The village Oued Laou, which is now a resort city, is located on the Laou River. The river runs sixty-five kilometers from its headwaters in the Rif Mountains, past the city of Chefchaouen, and into the Mediterranean at the city which is named for it.

We spent the next two weeks in Oued Laou camping on the beach. Every morning we would walk the short distance from Abdesalam's house to the river; then we would swing back around; walk down the beach; and watch the fisherman throw out their nets, which they would pull back in the late afternoon. The Med is sadly overfished and fishermen at Oued Laou usually had a pitiful catch of sardines, for which they had to work far too hard. Nonetheless, Rochma would turn the little fish into a tasty tajine with vegetables that were in ample supply. It was also just a short walk to the village oven where we picked up scrumptious fresh whole grain breads.

After lunch we would walk the fifty meters to the water's edge and roll out our beach mats, lay in the warm sun, and swim in the pleasant Mediterranean waters. If we got really ambitious, we would walk further down the beach to the large outcropping of rocks, hang out for a while, then return to the van for a proper Spanish siesta before watching the fishermen pull in their nets.

After dinner, we would sit on the roof of the small adobe home that Abdesalam built from mud and straw bricks. They would play drums, sing folk tunes, and tell folk tales. Abdesalam told us about '*debbles.*' *Debbles* apparently were Abdesalam's mispronunciation of the Spanish word *diablos* (or perhaps he meant devils or maybe *diablos* are devils.) In any case, *debbles* was such an amusing term that we never bothered to clarify precisely what he meant beyond the inference of a malevolent spirit of some sort.

He explained that the villagers in Oued Laou were simple people who believed in *debbles*, then he added, "I once saw a *debble* when I was young. It reached its hairy arm through the crack under the door and snatched a towel right out of my hands. However, I am now a college graduate, and I haven't seen a *debble* since I received my degree."

If there was ever a case for a university degree, this must be one of the more convincing.

Abdesalam continued to explain, "For example, people in this little village will not go over to the river at night because they say they have seen the *debbles* walking around over there. This is foolish. Rochma and I go there almost every night and we have never seen *debbles*."

While we were in Oued Laou, we always parked our VW van on the beach. One night we saw two ghostly white shapes coming from the river. For a moment I thought the villagers were right this time. Then the *debbles* passed by and headed into Abdesalam's house. The next morning, I asked Abdesalam if he had been to the river last night as usual.

"Of course," he replied, curious why I would ask the obvious. I then asked what he was wearing.

He smiled, "Well we were both wearing Rochma's covers as it is very misty along the river."

By 'Rochma's cover' he meant the white sheets that the women in Chaouen wrap over their heads and around their body. It is one of the striking features of Chaouen that you see all these 'Casper ghosts' walking about the whitewashed streets of the town. Every night, two of these 'Caspers' came out of Abdesalam's house and walked down the beach to the river. Perhaps it is no surprise that the villagers avoided that area.

I realize I shouldn't be too cynical about Moroccans' superstitions. God knows I have a few of my own. However, they did tend to explain every ache and pain in terms of someone having cast a spell on them.

Perhaps it's a matter of semantics. After all, psychologists will tell you that toxic relationships cause stress, and stress can cause illness. So, it probably doesn't matter if you call it 'bad vibes' or a 'curse;' the bottom line is it is bad for your health.

What is for sure, every time I laughed at Moroccans for being backward, they would have the last laugh. Anyway, we had a wonderfully refreshing time in Oued Laou. When it was over, we were ready to get back to Fez for the new school year.

Abdesalam also had to get back for his new school year, so he and Rochma joined us for the return trip. However, first they wanted to swing by the Moroccan side of the Ceuta border which at the time was a smuggler's paradise of European goods that can be purchased without the Moroccan import tax. As we approached Ceuta there was a long procession of Moroccans walking the other direction ladened down with everything from TVs, boom boxes to blankets. When we got into town we started going to electronic shops and Abdesalam and Rochma loaded up on things that were too expensive in Fez. It was becoming apparent that we were going to have a very active social life now that we had the van because most of the people we knew, Moroccan or American, didn't have cars and the van could carry a lot of stuff.

After Ceuta, we swung by Chaouen so Abdesalam could visit his father and sister, and Rochma could visit her mother and brother. Abdesalam's father was a retired watch maker and lived in one of the attractive whitewashed homes in the Chaouen *medina*. Rochma's mother was widowed and lived in a very modest dwelling in a small village near Chaouen. Rochma's mother prepared a lovely meal of fresh rabbit. When we complimented her, she said that we should thank her son because he was the hunter. I remarked that he must be a pretty good shot.

"No, I don't have a gun," he said, "I just chase them down."

Chasing down a rabbit is not an easy matter, made considerably more difficult by the rocky mountainous terrain of that area. It was not the only time I would be thinking to myself that Moroccans would make good distance runners, so I wasn't in the least bit surprised decades later when they started dominating the 1500 meters in world track competition. Likewise, we would see young boys playing soccer on nearly every vacant lot that we passed. We had pleasant visits with their families, then we continued to Fez, where we would be getting in late at night.

When we got to the Center the next morning, we learned that all the teachers were being sent to Rabat for the refresher course for English as a Second Language Instruction. This was the same course we took when we started teaching at the Language Center the year before. We welcomed the opportunity because we would get a *per diem*, making it a working vacation. We would finish early in the afternoon and have time to see Rabat with a car. We were also thinking it would be fun to check out some of Morocco's Atlantic coastline, right on the heels of our time along the Spanish and Moroccan Mediterranean coastlines.

Two days later we were up early and off to Rabat. Such adventures were so much more exciting after spending a year without a car. One of our students came along for the journey as he had relatives in Rabat that he hadn't seen for some time.

Rabat is about a hundred miles west of Fez and along the way you pass Meknes which is halfway. Meknes is one the former imperial cities, which is to say that a dynasty of Sultans based themselves there at one point in Moroccan history. Sultan Moulay Ishmael, the part monster, part master architect, had a building obsession that resulted in massive walls and palaces and many deaths.

On that occasion we had no business in Meknes, so we were merely taking the bypass to Rabat which skirted around Meknes. As we were passing Meknes, the van began to gasp, sputter and wheeze. We decided to try to make it into Meknes. The van hung on just long enough to get a couple of blocks from a garage before giving out completely. I went to the garage and fetched a couple of guys to help push the van to the garage. They agreed to look at it and suggested that we go get ourselves lunch, and hopefully they would have some answers by the time we finished eating. It was a nice day and we had little choice but to go with the flow. The Meknes *Ville Nouvelle* has a pleasant boulevard with comfortable outdoor cafes, and we ordered *brochettes* (kababs) for ourselves and Driss, the student who was with us.

It wasn't long before a tiny woman in a bright red vinyl raincoat with matching bonnet and bright yellow rubber boots came trudging down the sidewalk approaching each table, and each time the people laughed and shooed her away. Finally, she approached us. She was quite old with poorly applied crimson red lipstick and rouge caked on her cheeks. To say that her attire was distinctive would be a massive understatement - rather like as a cross between a bag lady and a circus clown. She spoke to us in French, and Driss explained, "She reads the cards, I'll ask her to leave."

However, Mary Ann said, "No, let her stay, it's not like we have anything else to do."

I pulled out a chair and 'Madame Clown' sat down and pulled out a deck of playing cards from her red vinyl bag. She shuffled the cards and laid out a few cards on the table three times. Each time she would pause to look at the cards then cock her head back and forth like a parrot, focusing on each one of us. Driss translated her French, but truthfully, I quickly lost interest and wasn't paying a whole lot of attention. It was a bunch of "this tall dark man will help you blah blah blah and this short blonde woman is to be watched out for." Then she cocked her head in my direction and stated that I would be somehow involved in espionage. She claimed that I was in danger but would be protected by a high military figure.

Right! As if I had all these dealings with military people and the rest seemed so general that it could have meant anything.

Then she startled me with, "But I suppose you are only interested in your car. Well, there is nothing wrong with it; you can pick it up now. You know things happen according to fate. If you hadn't had car problems you wouldn't be here talking to me, would you?"

I was bewildered that she knew anything about the car but figured she must have seen us push it into the garage. But was it true that the car was O.K.? We rushed back to the garage to check out her prediction and in fact the mechanic was holding the keys, saying, "I don't know, seems fine now," he said, "There was probably something in the gasoline line."

I spent a good deal of the drive into Rabat trying to rationalize how 'Madame Clown' knew so much about our van. For their part, Driss and Mary Ann weren't buying any of my efforts to deny that the old lady was psychic. It would be several years before I saw 'Madame Clown' again.

After we got back to Fez, we were busy at work and had to restrict our travels to the more immediate area, but we continued to research possible destinations and saved up money for a longer trip. Many people told us that their favorite scenery was the Draa River Valley leading to the small city Zagora, on the edge of the Sahara.

When the Language Center recessed for a winter break, we excitedly headed for the Sahara. Zagora is 410 miles from Fez, which in those days was an eleven-hour drive. We made it a two-day trip to Zagora, camping overnight mid-way and stopping frequently to enjoy the incredible hundreds of miles of river oases lined with towering *kasbahs*, made even more stunning by all the red peppers laid out to dry.

Near Zagora we stayed in a campground that was in a palm tree oasis along the river. The villagers prepared home cooked meals, fresh baked bread, and hand squeezed orange juice from a nearby orchard.

On our way back to Fez, we camped outside a small hillside village in the Middle Atlas Mountains. As the sun set over the hill, someone began playing an angelic flute. After a few minutes someone else on the other side of the village began playing an *oud* (a pear-shaped stringed instrument of the lute family). After a few more minutes, a drum began to beat. For the rest of the evening until quite late, more instruments joined in while others fell out from different locations as the village musicians put on their nightly Berber (Amazigh) Jazz concert.

A few months later we attended the Tangier Jazz Festival which was organized by the American jazz great Randy Weston who had taken up residence in Tangier. The festival featured many internationally famous jazz musicians, including Dexter Gordan and Hubert Laws, but the high point of the festival was when the Americans played a couple of sets with Moroccan Gnawa musicians. They were cookin' that night in Africa! Regardless, I preferred the spontaneous nightly jazz festival in the little Berber village.

Traditional architecture of southern Morocco

MOROCCAN MYSTIQUE

Ait Benhaddou

Atlas Mountains

5 - CHANGING OF THE GUARD

One day Chris called us into his office. He said that he was being reassigned as the Press Secretary at the Embassy in Beirut. The Center's new director would be a man by the name of Kenton Keith. He and his family would arrive in a few weeks. Chris told us how much he had enjoyed working with us and asked us to do everything possible to help the Keiths settle into Fez.

We had now been working for Chris for two years and we were concerned that his successor might not share Chris' commitment to us or the program. After all, the only reason we began working at the Center was because we had made a direct connection to Chris. Chris is a rare personality and it seemed unlikely he could be easily replaced.

As it turned out, Kenton is another powerful personality who went on to be the ambassador in Qatar. So, both of the directors of the American Cultural Center that I worked for in Fez would become ambassadors.

Kenton was one of the fastest rising African-Americans in the State Department. He was a former Navy officer and baseball player from Kansas State. His father played with the Count Basie jazz group and Kenton's contacts in the music world proved a powerful asset when he worked as the Cultural Attaché at the Istanbul and Cairo Embassies.

The first thing Kenton told us was that the student programs were **dead on** arrival.

"I congratulate you for the success of your programs, but you should know, in case you don't already, a high profile in this part of the world is not always a good thing. You have attracted the attention of people in high places, and they are uncomfortable with where all of this might be going. We will continue to bring in cultural programs but mostly just to amuse the high and mighty. Don't try and make Morocco into something it isn't. Let the change come from within. It is not our place to try and lead them. We will only make enemies. Just relax and enjoy your time here."

For a while I thought this was a cop-out. I felt that we were abandoning some very talented people, which in a sense, we were of course. But the more I thought about it, I realized that Kenton was right. Morocco needed to progress at its own pace. If we got too involved, we would just create problems. So, we turned our focus to providing technical support to Moroccan educational administrators. Unfortunately, or perhaps fortunately, the Moroccan administrators really didn't show much interest.

Kenton was an avid fisherman and was eager to see if any of the Atlas Mountain lakes had decent fishing. That also provided us an excuse to get out of town and enjoy the countryside. So, we turned some of our attention to fishing. Our favorite lake was coincidently the King's favorite fishing hole and part of the lake was inside a cyclone fence, which had a big sign. "This is His Majesty's Private Fishing Reserve - Unauthorized Fishing will be prosecuted to the full extent of the law" and the law in Morocco was usually quite painful.

Our most enthusiastic fisherman was a very talented Australian photographer by the name of Grant. He and his lady friend Jane had come to Morocco as tourists several years earlier. They were so intrigued by Fez they decided to stay longer than planned. They had their Australian bank forward a bank draft to a Moroccan bank. The process took so long that Grant had to take a job in a local photo lab just to survive. Eventually, he joined our team to handle the Center and the Embassy's photography.

Grant was a charming fellow and quite a character. When he went fishing, he always wore a red velvet sportscoat with the crest of the Melbourne Yacht Club. For Grant, fishing, like most things, was a gentlemen's sport to be executed with precision and humor.

One morning when Grant was getting nary a bite, he began to speculate that they surely stocked His Majesty's private reserve. Since we always got to the lake as the sun was coming up behind the mountains, we had the lake to ourselves and Grant decided to make his bold move to the King's Reserve, and the fishing improved immensely. Grant was also a gourmet cook and after our fishing trips he would serve everyone his specialty 'Poached Trout Royal.'

Besides fishing, Kenton's other passion was photography. That added even more talent to our graphic design team which was producing silk screened posters to advertise our English language courses and cultural events. One day USIS inspectors came through and we gave them a briefing on what we had been doing. Despite the lackluster response from the school administrators, our public relations package looked fantastic. The folks from Washington were apparently impressed by the Center's work and Kenton's charismatic personality; he was soon after promoted to the head position of USIS in Damascus, Syria. At the time, he was the youngest person to ever reach that level in the USIS.

However, the Center in Fez would likely be closed at an unspecified date. Mary Ann decided to return to school in the States and I chose to stay behind. Chris and Kenton devised a plan where I would go to Beirut and work part-time as a graphic artist in Beirut and part-time for Kenton in Damascus. I had always wanted to spend time in Beirut, but the arrangement would have required commuting through Lebanon's notorious Beqaa Valley, and the political situation in Lebanon was rapidly deteriorating. I decided to pass on the opportunity and see what was going to happen to the Center in Fez.

For the next three months, the Center remained in limbo. Naima,

Grant, and I sat in the Center drinking cappuccinos, talking, reading, and waiting for some word on what was going to happen with the Center. One day, the phone rang, and Naima was out so I picked it up. I recognized the voice of the head of USIS Morocco in Rabat, whom we called Big Bob.

"Who is this?" he wanted to know. I told him and he said, "Bill, what the hell are you doing there?"

"Oh not too much, what are you up to?" I replied.

"What I am trying to say, Bill, is you were taken off the payroll three months ago."

"Oh, I don't think so. Those checks keep coming in," I said.

"What about that Australian photographer?" he wanted to know.

"Oh, he is doing O.K., thanks."

"I can't believe you guys are still there. You better get down here tomorrow," he demanded.

Early the next morning Grant and I traveled the winding narrow road to Rabat. As usual, we enjoyed the lovely countryside and there was virtually no traffic, but I had to remain alert for horse and donkey-drawn carts that seemed to pop out of nowhere. We had one close call when we came around a bend and had to slam on the breaks because a couple of old country boys were sitting on the asphalt making tea. Who could argue with their logic? The road was perfectly flat and there was more than enough room for donkey carts to pass by. I sensed I wouldn't be making this drive too many more times, at least not for now.

In Rabat, we headed to the USIS offices and were led into Big Bob's plush office. We called him 'Big Bob' because he could be rather bureaucratic. Bob proceeded to tell us that we had been inadvertently overpaid three months' salary and we had to pay it back.

"How do you figure?" I asked.

"Well, what exactly have you done in the last three months?" Big Bob wanted to know.

"I didn't do anything. What did you ask me to do?"

"Well, I didn't ask you to do anything, but that isn't the point," he fired back.

"Actually, that is exactly the point, we followed your orders completely. Perhaps you would like to report our case to Washington? You know, tell them that you were paying two guys for three months and you thought they were gone. That can't look too good."

"O.K, O.K.," he conceded reluctantly, "Good Luck back home."

Islamic designs carved in plaster.

MOROCCAN MYSTIQUE

Melting Pot Club student produced magazine

MOROCCAN MYSTIQUE

Close-up of kilim runner from Middle Atlas

6 - TO OREGON AND BACK

After the fateful meeting with Big Bob, I needed some espresso before making the three-hour drive back to Fez, so Grant and I stopped by the café in Rabat's American Cultural Center, which was on the ground floor of the same building as Big Bob's office. We noticed that the Rabat Cultural Center's graphic artist Marlene was sitting by herself, so we joined her. She mentioned she was soon returning to the States on a Yugoslavian freighter that had a dozen passenger cabins. She gave me their phone number and I booked the last available cabin. It was leaving in a week. This was rather fortuitous as there wouldn't be another ship for six months and I wanted to return with my van and Moroccan carpets.

A week later I found myself at the Port of Casablanca going through Moroccan Customs. The unusually attentive customs agent checked my car papers against the serial number on the engine and found a discrepancy. Apparently, two years earlier, the used car dealer in Amsterdam sold us a stolen car and I didn't have the good sense to check the serial numbers. I had a big problem on my hands.

I told the customs man: 1) I am a humble teacher and a decent person; 2) I didn't steal the car; 3) it was stolen in Amsterdam, not really a Moroccan problem and finally (and perhaps most convincingly) I still had twenty dollars' worth of Moroccan dirhams that wouldn't do me any good in the States. He could do me a favor by taking my excess currency and forgetting the whole matter. Fortunately, Moroccans are practical people, and I was on my way.

It was a mostly wonderful ten-day cruise. We were a day late getting into New York because of detouring around a large storm. Consequently, we arrived on Labor Day weekend. Since they couldn't offload us on a holiday, we anchored a hundred yards from the Statue of Liberty, giving me three days to stare at the statue and contemplate my return to the Land of the Free.

When I got back to Oregon it was September 1974. I renewed my studies at the University of Oregon but changed my major from political science to graphic design. My time at the Cultural Center gave me some degree of confidence that I might be able to make a living employing my artistic talents. Shortly after returning I volunteered to help in the U.S. Senate campaign that was going on. Three years living in an absolute monarchy had enhanced my appreciation for the American democracy, despite its flaws. One day I went to a retirement center to pass out posters I had screen printed for my preferred candidate. An elderly lady took my poster and chucked it in the wastebasket.

"You know, young man, I don't need anybody to tell me who to vote for, I just need somebody to give me a ride to vote," she said, clearly challenging my sincerity (and party affiliation.) I could not pass on this 'put up or shut up' dare so I told her I would be back on Election Day. As it turned out, she had lots of friends, and I spent the day ferrying these old folks back and forth.

Apparently, somebody at the retirement center tipped off the newspaper that I was doing my civic duty and on one of my runs, a reporter and photographer were waiting for their story. I made the local newspaper, which effectively announced that I had returned home from my adventures. The next day I got a call from an old girlfriend whom I had known since high school, when we worked on the school newspaper together. Louise suggested that we have coffee and catch up on what we had been doing for these past few years. We began to date and would eventually get married.

I also reconnected with my best friend since the fourth grade. Bob Newland was a former All-American wide-receiver for the Oregon Ducks, who played professionally with the New Orleans Saints. Injuries ended Bob's very successful football career prematurely, and he became a lumber broker. He and I began to contemplate importing Moroccan crafts and carpets. At the end of that school year, Bob and his wife Christie; Louise and I; and my sister Jean and her husband Jim Grelle (who once held the American record in the mile run) put together a company called Newland Grelle Keenan Imports. Louise and I would return to Morocco as the buyers and my sister Jean would handle the marketing in Portland.

It was July of 1975. Louise and I flew ahead to Amsterdam and bought another van, and this time I made sure that the serial numbers matched. Unfortunately, I was so obsessed with the serial numbers that I failed to adequately check out the engine. Ironically, the engine failed just outside of Malaga, Spain where we were to meet the Grelles who were flying in to take a tour of Morocco with us. They delayed their departure from Portland for a few days and we stayed in the van at the garage that was rebuilding the engine. Malaga is a lovely city, but I wouldn't recommend staying in a garage.

When Jean and Jim arrived in Malaga, we took them up to Mijas, a fabulous little hilltop village, where they stayed at a lovely hotel overlooking the Costa del Sol. It was ridiculously cheap (those days are gone.) Jean mentioned that in anticipation of going to Morocco she had been doing some reading, but still had lots of questions. The glossary at the end of the book is a brief summary of the answers to Jean's questions, which others may also find helpful.

MOROCCAN MYSTIQUE

Berber kilim (*Amazigh hanbal*)

MOROCCAN MYSTIQUE

Jean Grelle at the cane weavers

Hassan Tower - Rabat

7 - CHEFCHAOUEN

A couple of days after Jim and Jean's arrival in Malaga, we loaded up the van and drove the short distance to Algeciras, where we caught a ferry to the small Spanish enclave of Ceuta on the Moroccan mainland east of Tangier. Perhaps you will notice a certain hypocrisy. The Spanish are furious about the Brits having the Gibraltar enclave on the Spanish mainland but have no intention of returning their Ceuta and Melilla enclaves to the Moroccans.

Our plan was to tour around Morocco, do some sightseeing and give Jim and Jean a sense of what was available in the way of carpets and handcrafts. We would do some light shopping and find out what hoops we had to jump through to start exporting. Our first stop was Chaouen, my friend Abdesalam's hometown.

Chaouen is one of the most beautiful cities in Morocco. It is nestled at the foot of the jagged basalt cliffs of the Rif Mountains of northern Morocco and the fresh mountain air is filled with the scent of cedar and fir trees. Chaouen was once Spanish Morocco and when we were there in 1975 its whitewashed adobe buildings with red tile roofs not surprisingly reminded us of Spain. The doors and windows were painted pale blue which was said to ward off the evil eye. The women drape themselves in white sheeting, so they seemed to blend into the buildings in a sea of whiteness. All that said, in recent times entire streets have been painted pale blue and Chaouen has become famously known as the Blue City.

There seem to be different theories on what caused this transformation. There was once a small Jewish neighborhood of refugees from the Spanish Inquisition in the 15th century who painted their houses blue, and some speculate that it spread from there. However, most of the Jews migrated to Israel in the 1940s and 50s, long before Chaouen became known as the Blue City. More likely the transition to blue was a result of Morocco's growing tourism industry and the fact that tourists were impressed by the streets that were painted blue, so the practice spread. For my tastes, Chaouen has gone a bit too far in the blue direction. I loved all the white with pale blue accents. I suspect in time they will tone down some of their use of the deeper blues. Regardless, Chaouen is a wonderful experience.

Chaouen's official name is Chefchaouen. *chef* is Arabic for 'he saw.' Chaouen is a reference to the mountain peaks behind the city that look like horns or antlers (or *ishwan* in the Tamazight dialect.) Everyone will understand if you call it Chaouen, just don't be confused if you hear someone say Chefchaouen.

We arrived in Chaouen shortly after a new hotel had opened on a hill overlooking the city. It seemed to have the best location in town, and I later asked Abdesalam why no one else hadn't already built there.

"Oh, that was a cemetery, none of us will live there - too many *djinn*," he explained.

At the hotel parking lot, we were greeted by two dwarfs in little red suits with pants that ended at the knee. They were also wearing the traditional long pointed yellow slippers and red fezzes. They looked like they had just stepped out of fairyland, but they were fighting over who would unload our car. After some heated squabbling, the two apparently worked out some arrangement and one of them scurried off. However, the remaining little bellboy couldn't hold the bags high enough to get them off the ground and soon we were fighting with him over who would carry them into the hotel. He won and dragged them on their sides across the still unpaved gravel parking lot, etching scratch marks into them as he went.

We checked in and he proceeded to drag the bags across the lobby to the elevator. He explained where the restaurant and the pool were, and then sternly cautioned us that we were strictly forbidden from using the hotel towels at the pool. Of course, we were incredulous at this ridiculous restriction.

"Do you think we brought pool towels with us from America?" Jim implored.

"Hey, look Mister, don't get mad at me, I am just little here."

"I see your point," Jim conceded with wry glances to the rest of us.

After a couple of days of wandering through Chaouen's charming *medina*, we left the peace and scenery of the Rif Mountains to meet with some exporters in Casablanca - a five-hour drive south.

Chaouen – The Blue City

Jean Grelle navigating the Chaouen *medina*

Traditional dress of Chaouen

Chaouen from our hotel

A little guy by a little door - Chaouen

Bill and Abdesalam's sister Fatima - Chaouen

8 - CASABLANCA

Casablanca is unlike the rest of Morocco. Although there has been a port at its location dating back to 10 A.D., it was never a large city until the French established it as their colonial and economic capital in the early 1930s. Consequently, the Casablanca *kasbah* is small and not a tourist attraction. Some of the older buildings the French built have attractive art nouveau and art deco architectural features, but the city really had no famous landmarks until the King Hassan II Grand Mosque was completed in 1993. It is one of the finest examples of Moorish architecture ever built, which is saying quite a lot. Two-thirds of the mosque is built out over the Atlantic Ocean and the coastline itself is quite pleasant with beaches, hotels, restaurants, and cafes. Given that most people fly into Casablanca, it may be well worth spending a day in Casablanca, rest up from the flight and visit the mosque. When we were in Casa in 1976 it was before the mosque was built, so once our business with the exporters was done, we planned to have a nice meal at one of the many fine French restaurants, get a good night's sleep and push on to Marrakesh.

In those days, the Moroccan economy was fairly closed to outside investment. There was an attitude of 'Well if this Westerner wants to do a certain business it might be something worth doing, so let's do it ourselves.' The result was usually that no one did it.

Consequently, there were legal restrictions against our doing our own exporting, so we would have to work with an established Moroccan exporter. Obviously, this created serious problems for us. For one thing, those established exporters were potential competitors and we didn't necessarily want them to do our buying. The other problem was that they wanted to work on a straight commission basis. This gave them a negative incentive to buy at a good price or more accurately, they could buy at a good price, then tell you that they paid 20% more than they actually had paid and then charge a 15% commission on top of that.

Not too surprisingly, we weren't jumping at the opportunity. Our only option was to help a Moroccan that we knew and trusted get an export license. We decided to go ahead with our tour and worry about finding our export partner when we got to Fez.

Shop in the Casablanca *kasbah*

Hassan II Grand Mosque - Casablanca

9 – MARRAKESH AND THE SOUTH

The next morning, we had a wonderful breakfast at the hotel, packed up and headed for Marrakesh. It was a two-and half-hour drive and one of the few drives in Morocco that isn't in the least bit scenic. The good news was that we were closing in on one of the premier tourist destinations in the world, so we were sufficiently excited that the time flew by.

Marrakesh is the gateway to the Sahara, and it has an incomparable air of intrigue associated with its proximity to the world's largest desert. The iconic Koutoubia Mosque's tall minaret overlooks Jemaa el-Fnaa, the open square market with its lively mix of food stands, snake charmers, storytellers, and Gnawa musicians and dancers. The square is surrounded by cafes and restaurants and is adjacent to the *medina*. It is a living theater that plays every day.

The large and colorful *medina* is home to wonderful examples of Moorish architecture, such as the Badi Palace, and Medersa Ben Youssef. Its shops and bazaars carry a variety of high-quality traditional crafts, making Marrakesh a unique shopping experience.

Marrakesh is called the Red City due to its terracotta-colored walls and buildings which are surrounded by palm groves and backdropped by the nearby snow-capped High Atlas Mountains. It is a stunning setting.

Not surprisingly Marrakesh has three million tourists a year (as of 2020.) and Europe's rich and famous have built large homes in the nearby palm groves and renovated the elegant traditional *riads* (homes built around an atrium garden) in the *medina*. There has been an explosion of new hotels, most of them in harmony with the city's Moorish desert style.

Despite all of this, one of my most lasting impressions of Marrakesh will always be the young belly dancer who rolled around on the floor with a large brass tray carrying a couple dozen tea glasses and a teapot balanced on her head. Then she gracefully rose to a standing position and filled the glasses which were now sitting on the floor four feet below - of course, all without spilling a drop. I thought about all the little girls I had seen with a four-foot-long board stacked with fresh bread dough balanced on their heads as they gracefully weaved their way through the crowds on their way to the neighborhood ovens.

Another lasting impression from Marrakesh came from the day we sat in a café with an enclosed patio. We were having our lunch and a boy selling postcards started pressing us to buy his product. As there are dozens of these kids running around, we were already up to our necks in postcards, but as so often was the case, the young fellow just wouldn't bug off. Never one to be intimidated, Jim began to shake and quiver like an epileptic. Of course, Jim was not aware of how superstitious the Moroccans are and how the young boy would perceive his antics.

The boy froze, giving Jim a look of shock and horror. Clearly, he thought Jim was possessed by *djinn*. Then in a fit of panic, he threw his cards up in the air, jumped on our table, and scaled the wall as he made his quick escape from the restaurant. Jim acknowledged the polite applause of our fellow tourists who had also been driven crazy by these street salesmen who stuck to you like glue. As relieved as I was to get rid of the boy, I could not help but feel sorry that he had abandoned his stockpile of postcards that some souvenir shop had undoubtedly provided on a commission basis. These little guys often put dinner on the family's table and now he would spend the next couple of months trying to pay off his losses.

After Marrakesh, we headed east into the Atlas Mountains. Along the road there were men selling crystals, rose quartz and geodes as big as three feet high. The men were still wearing the white and brown *djellabas* we had seen elsewhere, however in the mountains the Amazigh women were unveiled and wore brightly decorated scarves and black capes accented by necklaces of huge amber beads and silver coins. They were stunning.

In Ouarzazate, Jean and Jim checked into a fashionable hotel, and we camped in the parking lot. Ouarzazate is just 30 miles from Ait Benhaddou, which is one of the best-preserved Amazigh *kasbahs*. Its intricately decorated mud clay towers take the visitor back to the 11th century, when the Amazigh Almoravid Dynasty had an empire with its capital in Marrakesh that included present day Morocco, Mauritania, and half of Spain. Due to the amazing *kasbahs* in the area (also referred to as *ksars* which means castle in Arabic) many movies have been filmed here and Ouarzazate has become known as the 'Moroccan Hollywood.'

After a day of touring the Ouarzazate area, we moved on to Er-Rashidiyyah, which was called Ksar el-Souk (Castle of the Market) at the time we were there in 1975. The next morning, we departed well before the sun came up in hope of taking advantage of the relatively cool morning temperature as we began our trek down to Rissani, on the edge of the Sahara. Rissani is the end of the road. After that it is just the sand dunes of the world's largest desert. Rissani is known for its excellent silver and amber jewelry. The nomadic Amazigh tribes come off the desert as far as Rissani and exchange their goods for some of their necessities. Much of the drive to Rissani went through a beautiful river oasis with old *kasbahs* lining the road.

After a few hours, both Jim and I were getting tired because of our early departure from Ksar el Souk. Also, the sun had come up, the temperature was rising quickly, and the van didn't have air conditioning. We asked Jean to take over at the wheel while we snoozed in the back. She happily obliged. Jim and I slipped into a deep sleep. After an hour in dreamland, I was awakened by Jean shrieking and the van coming to a jerking halt. I popped up and looked around. We were surrounded by sand dunes. Jean had come around a corner and she ran into a sand dune that had blown across the road.

We got out and assessed our predicament. Jean said she hadn't seen another car the entire time that she was at the wheel - not a good sign. Fortunately, we had water, but we knew it would start getting extremely hot in another hour or two. I was sure we would eventually see someone come along, but they would be in the same situation that we were. At that moment, two young guys popped out from behind the dunes with shovels in their hands. They said for the equivalent of $10 they would clear enough of the road for us to get by. We couldn't help but admire these innovative entrepreneurs. We wondered whether they followed the road every day looking for where the wind had done its work, or did it always happen at this one spot, and they had learned that this was the spot to go into business? We even considered the possibility that as soon as we left that they would start shoveling the sand back onto the road.

In 1976 Rissani was a little dust bowl of a place. The town square consisted of about ten shops on each side. Outside on the sidewalks, the women had spread out their wares, mostly Amazigh silver jewelry. In years past there had been a silver mine nearby, which is why Rissani had become well known for silver jewelry. The sales ladies were all African ladies wearing black *abayas* like those worn by women in Saudi Arabia. I read that these women were part of a relatively large Jewish population that inhabited the Rissani-Erfoud area.

I personally love Amazigh jewelry. The women in the Atlas Mountains cover themselves in vests made of silver coins and necklaces of huge beads of red and yellow amber. We would try to buy these lovely pieces to sell as collector pieces, but more often had to break them down into smaller necklaces that American women would be more likely to wear.

We then moved on to the carpet *souks* (markets.) The carpets in this region were generally thick pile tribals, not fine by knot count, but splendid designs. We picked a shop that had some particularly beautiful pieces hanging out front. Inside the owner was already involved with an older Moroccan man in a white *djellaba* and white turban. One of the assistants brought us the traditional fragrant and much too sweet mint tea.

As we sipped our tea and waited our turn, we noticed that the old Moroccan would take each carpet and lift an edge to within a half inch of his eye. Jean asked me what he was looking at. I confessed that I wasn't sure. My carpet expertise was still a work in progress. I knew what I liked but that was about it.

"He seems to be getting a real good look at the fiber of the wool. I know how to burn a little thread and you can tell from the smell if it is pure wool. But he seems to have another technique. I will ask around and see if I can find out what he is looking for," I offered weakly.

Finally, after much haggling, the old man and the owner agreed on a carpet and a price, and the old guy reached into his *djellaba* and pulled out some neatly folded bills. But when he got his change back, he took each bill and ran it within a half inch of his eye. It suddenly became obvious he was nearly blind. Jim nearly choked on his tea and gave me a high five.

"Maybe you shouldn't spend too much time trying to learn this technique after all," Jim chuckled.

We went back to Ksar el-Souk for the night and then visited Tinghir and the Todgha Gorge the next morning. This area has some of the most beautiful scenery in all of Morocco - and that is saying quite a bit.

Jemaa el Fnaa Square - Marrakesh

Koutoubia Mosque - Marrakesh

Marrakesh outer walls

Marrakesh – the Red City

10 - THE EXPORT BIZ

After arriving in Fez, Jean and Jim checked into the Merinides Hotel, which is perched on a cliff above the *medina* with an wonderful view. I went up to the *Ville Nouvelle* where the American Cultural Center was located. Although I expected the Center to be empty, it was at least a starting point in my search for an export partner. Amazingly, as I approached the front office, I saw Naima locking the door. She couldn't believe it. She had been there for the last nine months as the only employee, as they waited for the lease to run out and finally decided what to do. Naima was locking up for the last time. The Center was officially closed, and she was out of a job. The synchronicity of my returning to the Center at the very moment Naima was locking the door for the last time was not lost on either of us.

Naima was on my short list of prospective export partners. In many respects, Abdesalam was a natural choice, we were close friends, he was imminently trustworthy, and of course he was a man. Unfortunately, he had his teaching job and we needed someone's full attention. There was also the matter that Naima's husband was now the Chief of Gendarme for the Fez region (i.e., Chief of the State Police.) Contacts are everything in Arab countries and Naima had them. Besides her husband's position, Naima was a Belghiti, a highly respected Fez family, and her brother in Casablanca was the head of IBM-Morocco. Abdesalam by contrast was a Ketami, the tribe from Ketama, the hashish growing region in the Rif Mountains. I had already learned that setting up an export business in Morocco was not going to be easy. Trying to do it with a Ketami was asking for even more obstacles. So, for those reasons, along with the fateful encounter with Naima the very moment that she locked up the Center for the last time, we concluded that Naima was the right person to be our Moroccan partner.

After Naima accepted our proposal, she invited us to a lunch at her home to celebrate the launch of the business and work out more details. Jim had been having a wonderful time at the hotel swimming pool overlooking the *medina*, so we told him to hang out there and we would schedule a taxi to pick him up in a couple of hours. A couple of hours later we got a call from the taxi driver saying that Jim wasn't answering the phone in his room or the page for him at the pool. I asked the driver to swing by and get me and I would go see what was going on. When I got to Jim's room, he was sitting on the floor in the hallway with a towel wrapped around his waist.

I said, "Jim, even for being the most eccentric person I know, you have me baffled this time."

Jim explained that he had taken a shower, however when he finished, he discovered that all the towels were wet. So, he looked out in the hallway and there was a housekeeping cart just a couple of doors down. He wrapped a wet towel around himself and dashed to the cart to grab a dry towel. Just as he got to the cart the wind slammed the door to his room shut. A maid eventually came out of a room, but she said she didn't have a key to Jim's room, and she would have to go to the desk to get it. After a bit, she returned and said they couldn't find the key. This was all a bit hard to believe, so I went to the desk and had a chat with the desk clerk. The problem was that the night before Jim had a bad migraine and had run out of bottled water. During Jim's days as an international track star, he learned the hard way to never drink anything but bottled water. Unfortunately, room service didn't appreciate the urgency of the situation and Jim got testy with the desk clerk. So, the 'missing key' was all about payback. Anyway, everything got resolved, apologies were exchanged, and most importantly the door was opened. We made it back to Naima's in time for lunch and everyone had a good laugh about the slamming door at the Merinides

Hotel.

As we lunched on a delicious multicourse Moroccan feast, we began to work out more details of the new partnership. Naima mentioned that she still kept her late mother's apartment for sentimental reasons. She said Louise and I could stay there when we were in Fez, store merchandise, and prepare shipments.

With the export partnership nailed down we did a little more traveling with the Grelles before they flew back to Portland where Jean began to look for a location to open our carpet store.

The fact that Naima quickly got her export license, becoming the first Moroccan woman to ever do so, convinced me that we made right decision, as much as it pained us to hurt Abdesalam's feelings. Nonetheless, I was also aware that there would inevitably be issues associated with having a female partner. On our first day, as Naima and I were walking about from one government office to another, a couple of men cast aspersions at Naima's honor. We ignored them, but I asked how her husband felt about her running about town with me.

"Don't worry," she said, "You have my husband's complete trust."

"I do?" I asked, somewhat surprised at her overwhelming certainty.

"Of course, he has had you under surveillance for three years."

I could tell she was serious. Although, my position at the Center had been low level, the mere fact that I worked with the U.S. Government made me someone to keep an eye on. In Morocco labor is cheap and informants are recruited in large numbers. It was said there was a government informant in every café monitoring dissent, so arguably everyone was under surveillance. We heard stories about a group of French teachers who got a knock on the door and a 24-hour deportation notice, as result of critical observations that they had made at a café. I also flashed back to the tarot card reading I had with

'Madame Clown' in Meknes. Perhaps her comments about espionage were not so ridiculous after all.

I also understood that if Moroccan women were to make real progress in the workplace that they had to have the confidence of their husbands and fathers. I was proud that our company was helping break ground in giving a woman an opportunity in business. As for the hecklers, she ignored them knowing that word travels fast in Fez and soon enough everyone in town would know that she had one of those rare export licenses. Besides, if they gave her too much trouble, she could always have her husband throw them in jail.

Not long after she got her export license Naima invited us to a baby shower.

"You know I would never pass up a Moroccan feast, but I thought these events were only for women," I asked her, rather puzzled where this was going.

She gave us her patented mischievous smile, "Well you made me the first woman to get an export license, why shouldn't I make you the first man to attend a baby shower?"

What could I say?

All the ladies at the party liked the idea of Naima turning the tables on me and they showed us a great time. After we ate, the drums came out and there was singing and dancing. I was sitting on a banquette with women on each side of me. After a bit I couldn't resist the hypnotic drum rhythms, I closed my eyes, swayed back and forth, and sailed way. When the music stopped, I opened my eyes and Naima was laughing.

"I think you like the ladies' party, don't you?"

One of Naima's other great assets was that she knew a network of lady carpet weavers. Although much of the carpet weaving was done in large factories, there are scores of women who have established their own cottage industries with anywhere from one to a dozen looms. They bring in neighborhood girls and train them, and the lady weavers are generally more humane than the large factories.

Most of the weavers in Morocco are girls ten to sixteen years old. They learn incredibly complicated designs by memorization and work at speeds so fast that you can barely see their fingers moving. In the factories, there are often older girls that go around with a stick and wonk them on the head if they start slowing down or visiting too much. It is sad to think that so many girls spend their childhood this way, and even sadder to think how the families could not get by without the money. The lady weaver who we bought our carpets from was in fact once one of those girls working in the factory. She learned the business from the ground up, and after she got married, she started working out of her house and eventually was able to hire several girls herself.

Some people back home suggested that we were taking advantage of these girls by buying the carpets that they made. The truth is that we eventually lost money on our adventure. Surely some of that was our own fault, but the fact is that even though we were able to keep our costs down by going directly to the weavers, in those days people in Oregon were reluctant to put down money for a Moroccan carpet as opposed to a Persian or even more likely a machine-made carpet. Unfortunately, we were about fifty years ahead of our time, as Moroccan Berber carpets are wildly popular today. (These are the white pile carpets with black diagonal stripes, sometimes referred to as Beni Ouarain.)

I think it is safe to say that the girls had high hopes that we would succeed. They wanted job security, and our independent weaver paid better wages than they could get from the large factories. Of course, we wanted to make a profit, but we also knew that if we succeeded that it would be positive for the Moroccan economy and its people.

Americans rightfully object to the whole idea of child labor but the truth is everything about poverty is objectionable. In the end the solution is economic development. Only when the parents can afford to send the kids to school will you be able to really tackle the problem. My own opinion is that overpopulation is the real devil. When poor people from poor countries have lots of kids, society will usually have difficulty in educating all of them.

Interestingly, after our first carpet purchase, the lady weaver didn't immediately agree to selling more carpets. After a couple of weeks, she called us in and said we could purchase more carpets. She told me, "Now I know you have good money."

I told Naima that I didn't understand, "Isn't all money good money?"

Naima said that not all Moroccans would agree with that characterization.

"Sometimes money can cause problems. For example, a person might come into some money, so they buy a car, then have an accident. That person might conclude that the car was purchased with bad money. The weaver waited until she was confident that our money wasn't going to cause her any trouble."

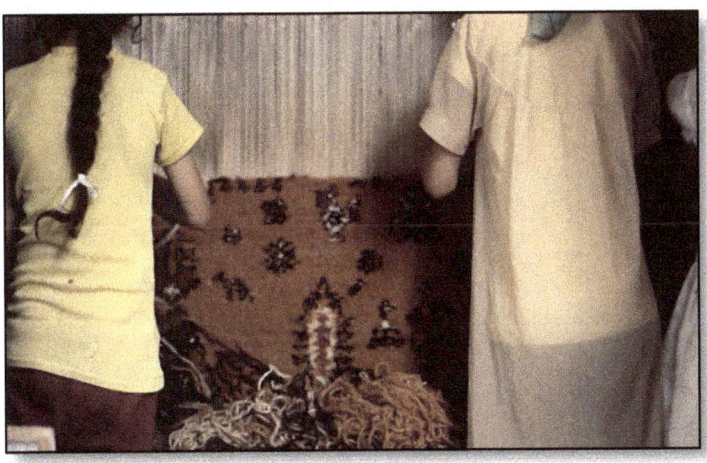

Girl weavers - Fez

Bennis serving mint tea at Naima's partnership lunch

Silver jewelry market - Rissani

Jean and Jim Grelle stranded in the Sahara

River oasis near Erfoud

11 - THE SHAWAFA

One weekend Naima, Louise and I were walking near one of the gates to the *medina* in Fez and we saw several Moroccan women sitting in front of the walls giving tarot readings. I told Naima about 'Madame Clown,' the tarot reader in Meknes. Naima said that she would be curious to see her. I responded that I didn't know how to reach her, and we couldn't exactly make an appointment.

Naima said, "Well, if she is as psychic as you suspect we don't need an appointment."

I agreed and we planned a day trip to Meknes and the surrounding area. First, we would swing by the two-thousand-year-old Roman ruins at Volubilis for a picnic. Then we would drive over to the holy city of Moulay Idriss Zerhoun, where the Muslim Arabs established their first settlement in Morocco in the late 8th century. Then we would drive back through Meknes and drive down the boulevard to see if 'Madame Clown' was working the outdoor cafes.

Louise and I often visited Volubilis because we were usually by ourselves, and we could picnic wherever we wanted in peace. We would pour water on the ancient mosaic floors, and they would come alive. Surprisingly, Naima's husband Drihany, the Chief of the Gendarme, said he would like to come along. This was quite unusual for him as his work kept him very busy. The Holy Shrine of Moulay Idriss Zerhoun was probably too much to pass on.

Driving back through Meknes, Naima did indeed spot 'Madame Clown' in her bright red vinyl coat straggling down the street with matching plastic bags in tow. Naima excitedly asked me to pull over, but Drihany was insistent that we move on and not involve him in this nonsense. But of course, Naima prevailed. I pulled over and helped 'Madame Clown' into the back of the van. Drihany ducked down in hopes that no one would see the Fez Chief of the Gendarme engaging this strange little lady.

She gave Naima a quick reading and we helped her down from the van. However, before we shut the door, she stuck her head back in, peered at Drihany, cocking her head back and forth, then she looked at me and confidently declared, "That's him, he's the military man that I told you about. He is the one who has been protecting you."

Drihany was of course in civilian clothing and quite taken back that she knew he was a high-ranking military man. (In Morocco, the gendarme is for all practical purposes part of the military.) I was just as surprised as Drihany that she knew what he was, but I was equally surprised that despite the hundreds of customers she had in the previous four years she would remember me and what she had said to me. I was left wondering if she was relying on something beyond conventional powers of recall. It would not be the last time I would see 'Madame Clown.' For her part, Naima was quite amused by what had transpired. I asked how her reading went.

"She is good but only time will tell how good. One of these days I'll take you to a lady in Casablanca who is amazing."

A few weeks later, Louise became aware that two of her rings were missing. We mentioned it to Naima on account of all the traffic coming and going from the apartment. Naima was visibly upset and said it was definitely time to go to Casablanca and visit the *shawafa* and get to bottom of this. We asked who or what the *shawafa* was and Naima explained that a *shawafa* was a Moroccan psychic who would go into a trance and answer questions, remove spells, protect one from the evil eye or provide advice.

"The *shawafa* who we will see is a very powerful one. My sister and I have seen her many times. I will call Rashida and make sure the *shawafa* is able to see us next week."

We also wanted to visit the largest hand-woven carpet manufacturer in Morocco which was in Casa. We hoped at the very least we could compare prices and designs. So, our plan was to spend several days and visit Naima's two brothers as well.

Rashida and her newlywed husband Abdulatif had a lovely new apartment just off a beautiful grass lined boulevard that was filled with gardens and palm trees. Discovery of this neighborhood did a lot to improve my impression of Casablanca. The next morning, I decided to stretch my legs and experience the boulevard by taking a run. The ladies said that was a great idea because they wanted to shop for groceries. and we could meet back at the apartment in an hour.

It was a beautiful sunny Casablanca morning, but I wore my sweats nonetheless as Moroccans in those days were not accustomed to seeing people running in the streets, and certainly not in shorts. (Today they have the best runners in the world.) I had been running for about ten minutes when I came upon a government building with two policemen standing guard on the sidewalk. They immediately drew their weapons and demanded that I halt. To say that I was startled would be quite an understatement.

The policemen checked to see if I was armed and then demanded see my ID, Unfortunately, I left my passport at Rashida's apartment because I didn't want to drench it in sweat while I was running. At this point I realized that I was at the entrance to the U.S. Consulate, and it was starting to dawn on me that the policemen were concerned that I might be a potential threat to the Consulate. They asked why I was running, and I told them it was for exercise. They seemed unconvinced by my explanation, and regardless, they explained it was illegal to be out in public without ID, exercising or not. They would have to detain me at a nearby police station for further questioning. I spent a moment trying to diffuse the incident with wit and charm, but they weren't buying it.

At the very moment all hope was lost, and I started contemplating what a day or two, or more, in a Moroccan prison was going to be like, a black limo pulled into the driveway. I could see a blonde lady in the back seat, and I started waving my hands and then gathered them in prayer. The limo came to a stop and the lady rolled down her window.

"Are you American?" she asked.

"Yes Ma'am, and I am in serious need of consular help."

She said she was the Consul General and wanted to know what the problem was.

After I explained, she said, "This should be easy to resolve. My driver will take you and a policeman to your friends' apartment to get your passport. Will your friends be home?"

"Well, the ladies may still be shopping but the maid can let me in. Thank you so much, you have been an enormous help." I said sighing with relief.

"Not a problem, just remember this ain't Peoria. Keep your passport on you at all times."

When we got to the apartment the policemen knocked on the door and after a moment Rashida's little maid Aicha opened the door. You could see the panic grip her face when she saw the policeman. He asked Aicha if she knew me.

"Sir, I swear by God, I have NEVER seen this man."

Terrific, now I was sure the police were going to throw me in the dungeon and throw away the key. The policeman grabbed me by the arm and led me downstairs and was putting me in the back seat of the limo. At that very instance, Naima, Louise, and Rashida pulled up in a taxi. Naima jumped out and explained that she was my friend and the wife of the Chief of the Gendarme in Fez and wanted to know what was going on. They talked for a moment, then Naima told Rashida and Louise to go up and get my passport. Naima and the policeman continued to talk and laugh, and I was starting to feel like the episode was over. I say 'over,' except for the fact that Naima had to repeat the hilarious story to everyone in Casablanca, much at my expense.

The following morning, we pulled into a shanty town on the outskirts of Casablanca. The children swirled around the van and tugged at our clothing, some wanting to exchange pleasantries, others demanding money. Naima shooed them away very kindly. We entered one of the shacks. There were women sitting on little rickety benches lined up against the walls. It looked like a doctor's office for the indigent. As soon as we entered there was a big ruckus.

"What are these *nazaranis* (Christians) doing here?" one woman demanded.

"Get them out of here before the *djinn* leaves!" another insisted.

Naima tried to reassure them but there was more loud protesting. Finally, a woman of about thirty appeared from a side room and everything quieted. She and Naima embraced. Naima pointed to us, and they talked a moment, then Naima introduced us. The *shawafa's* name was Zahara. Then Zahara turned to the women on the benches, "These *nazaranis* are Naima's friends, so they are my friends. They want to know more about our customs. They are welcome, if you have a problem with that you can leave, but don't come back. Everyone quietly sat down, and the glances turned mostly friendly.

As I was looking around the room to get a better sense of the *shawafa's* clientele, a young man of around twenty came out from the side room and said we were next. We went into the small dark room. Zahara was now sitting on the floor in front of a candle and large incense burner and projecting a very different presence. The young man, who I was later to learn was her brother, stood at the door. The room was already thick with smoke and the scent of sandalwood, but she added several more pieces to her incense burner. She slowly covered her head with a white gauzy veil. Her face was now barely visible. Then she put on numerous necklaces of shells and beads. Suddenly she jerked back and began to wail, then moan or shriek.

Then in a strange voice speaking an Amazigh dialect, she asked Naima if she had a question. Naima explained that Louise and I lived in her mother's apartment, and we had two rings go missing. We wanted to know what happened to them.

Zahara explained that Louise was sitting in the living room when 'five' rings were taken. Zahara said that Louise thought something odd was going on in the bathroom but did not follow up on her hunch. Zahara said Louise had left two rings out on the counter and three more in a small pouch on the shelf. She said that Naima's twelve-year-old maid Malika, had taken them. When we got back to the van, we told Naima we shouldn't jump to conclusions until we confronted Malika. Naima said she had known Zahara for several years; if Zahara said Malika took the rings, you could be sure that was what happened.

On our return to Fez, the first thing we did was to check to see if the *shawafa* was correct that five rings had been stolen, not just the two that we asked about. And indeed, in addition to the two rings that Louise left out on the counter next to the sink, three more were missing from the pouch that was on a shelf. Two were Louise's and one was mine.

Louise observed, "It seems the *shawafa* is doing a better job of looking after our things than we are."

When Naima confronted Malika, she denied everything. Naima told Malika she would talk to her husband Drihany when he got home before deciding what to do.

Louise and I had a lot of sympathy for Malika. Her parents lived in very humble conditions in a small mountain village, and it was common for young girls like Malika to be placed as maids with wealthier Fezi families. Naima was a kindhearted woman who treated Malika well. Nonetheless, Malika was spending her childhood working as a maid rather than going to school. She slept on a foam mattress in the kitchen, but she was well fed, and protected. She was also experiencing the world beyond the mountain village.

Naima was fastidious about keeping everything in her house under lock and key and had previously told us that she had problems with the maids stealing in the past. It wasn't hard to understand why a little girl of Malika's background might think Louise and I had too much stuff if we left jewelry lying around the bathroom. We had been careless and placed a temptation in front of child who was not prepared for it.

I was reminded that Louise once told me that her grandfather, who worked in Saudi Arabia for decades, had some of his workers steal his tools. Knowing that they were superstitious, he told them that these tools had a hex on them and a day later the tools miraculously reappeared. I thought I would try this approach on Malika.

One of the rings that Malika had taken was given to me by the late Bernie Worrell, who was a Music Hall of Famer and keyboardist for the Funkadelics, and later Talking Heads. I told Malika that my ring was given to me by a magician. That was only a minor exaggeration. Anyone who ever heard Bernie Worrell play understands that he did magic with a keyboard. There is also the matter that a few years earlier I had been backstage while the Funkadelics were warming up for a London concert. I witnessed them employ the same kind of trance inducing African tribal rhythms that we would later see with the Gnawa musicians in Morocco.

Within an hour Malika came running in, and surprise, surprise, she had found Bernie's ring while she was cleaning the kitchen. She speculated that someone else must have hidden it there. I thanked Malika for returning the ring and told her she was off the hook with Bernie the Magician, but she still had a problem with not telling the truth and returning all the jewelry. Again, she denied any involvement. I patiently explained to her that Louise and I really liked her and were sympathetic to the fact that she was still very young and had a difficult life. I said if she would just tell the truth she could put the matter behind her. However, if she refused to tell the truth Louise and I could not protect her from the consequences. Again, she denied being involved.

A couple of hours later Drihany returned home while we were still there. He lined up Malika and demanded the truth. Malika still refused to fess up. Drihany quickly decided that Malika needed to return home to her parents.

The very next day Naima, Louise, Malika, and I headed off to the foothills of the Middle Atlas Mountains to meet with Malika's parents. It was a lovely November day, which in the Fez region meant mild temperatures and an invigorating freshness in the air. The hills were green and men in donkey drawn carts full of vegetables were on the side of the road headed for market. The road climbed gently for about an hour before we turned into a small valley that led up to a small village of about thirty nearly identical homes. The homes were surrounded by high walls that were constructed from mud bricks the same color as the soil, causing them to blend into the hillside. The little mountain colony appeared immune to the passage of time. Malika tepidly directed us to her parents' home. We pulled up alongside the house and Malika's mother came out and greeted us. Inside the walls there was a courtyard surrounded by animal sheds, with a small door entering the house. We were led up the stairs to the second floor sitting room, where we were served fresh bread with wild honey and of course mint tea.

The room was plain but quite attractive with a high ceiling, round wood beams, and tall windows that surrounded the room on three sides. The windows did not have glass and the shutters were open to the fresh air. Naima and the mother exchanged pleasantries for a while, then began discussing Malika's situation. Stealing is a very serious crime in Muslim countries. In more conservative countries a third time offense might cost a thief his or her hand. However, Malika was twelve years old and the only evidence against her was the testimony of a *shawafa*. That said, in Morocco the testimony of some *shawafas* is admissible in court and Malika's mother understood that Naima was a sincere individual. Naima told Malika's mother not to overreact. It was punishment enough that she had been sent home. This made sense to Malika's mother, and she said Malika could be replaced by one of her cousins.

The successful resolution of the problem called for cookies and more mint tea. After a while we heard a man shouting in the courtyard. Naima said that they wanted us to see something. We went over to the open windows and leaned out. Malika's father was in the courtyard with a ram on a leash. Upon seeing us he picked up a long knife, bent the ram's head back and slit its throat. Without a peep, the ram collapsed to its knees and then fell over. The father then cut a slit in the ram's side and proceeded to blow into it until it was bloated, then he pulled the hide off the corpse. The ram was then roasted. The process took longer than we had expected to stay but Naima explained that this was the family's way of saving face from Malika's bad behavior. Besides, the roasted ram was well worth waiting for. That evening we made our way down the mountains with Naima and her new little maid Fatima.

A few weeks later a friend from Oregon paid a visit. Kate was accompanied by her friend David, who was getting his master's degree in architecture at the University of Oregon. David's father owned malls in Chicago and David wanted to do a photographic project on Morocco's distinctive style of displaying vegetables, fruits, and spices.

During the visit, we told Kate and David about our encounter with the *shawafa,* and they both expressed interest in seeing her. We told Naima that our friends would like to see the *shawafa*, and Naima said she also had some things on her mind and would try to arrange something. A few days later we all packed ourselves in the van and made the little over three-hour drive to Casablanca, stopping at a roadside kabab stand. David is a vegetarian, so he made do with tabouli and bread.

Once again, we stayed with Naima's sister Rashida. Rashida's apartment had a large *majlis* with copious banquettes lining the walls. So, it was a bit of a slumber party `a la Marocaine. Naima and Rashida went out of their way to prepare vegetarian meals for David although they didn't really understand the whole vegetarian thing.

In the morning we had a traditional Moroccan breakfast, then made our way over to the shanty town and pulled up in front of the *shawafa's*. This time the women in the waiting room had been warned we were coming and greeted us warmly as we went directly into the small side room, made even smaller by the addition of Kate and David. Zahara had already begun her rituals of covering herself with shells and gauzy scarves. As before the room was thick with sandalwood smoke and there was a small candle on the floor.

We had barely sat down before Zahara began to moan, shriek, and speak in a very bizarre voice. David had already seen and heard enough; he jumped up and headed for the exit. However, Zahara's brother stepped in the way of the door and stated the rules; no one is permitted to leave at this stage. David is a black belt karate champion, but he reluctantly acquiesced and sat back down. Zahara continued with her wailing and shrieking for a couple more moments and then went silent. Then she said something to Naima. Naima then whispered to David that this was about him. Zahara proceeded to explain that David had lived in a European port while in a relationship with a woman who was older than he - David was only twenty-two. Zahara then advised David that his lady friend was a witch who had put a spell on him. Consequently, no woman would take him seriously until the spell was removed.

David later told us that in fact he had lived with such a woman in Amsterdam and that he was having trouble establishing another relationship since their breakup, this even though he was buff, devilishly handsome and wealthy. None of us really knew David all that well and details of his love life were news to us.

Next Zahara turned her attention to me, "You arrived in Fez several years ago. On your first day in Fez, you gave the last of your money to the poor and then went to the Shrine of Moulay Idriss. Moulay Idriss gave you his stamp. Because of this, you will always be well taken care of in Morocco. However, there is one problem; you led Naima and her family to believe that you and Louise were married. That is a lie, and you must stop this charade.

Zahara then stated that I still had strong feelings for a woman that I had been in love with, but it was over. The other woman had gotten married, and I must as well. Besides Louise was a better match for me. She was from my tribe and would do anything for me and my family. It was in fact true that at my suggestion Louise and I told everyone that we were married. I simply felt in Morocco's conservative society that would make things far less complicated.

Zahara then turned to Kate and said that she was a divorcee and unhappy. Her friendship with David was never going to be any more than a friendship and it would be some time before she settled down. In the meantime, she had to learn to make herself happy by herself.

Finally, Zahara said she wanted to talk to Louise privately, so her brother led me outside. I took the opportunity to ask the brother for a little more information about his sister's powers.

"My father was a very well-known psychic. His powers came from a *djinn* who possessed him. When my father passed away a number of years ago, the *djinn* moved to Zahara, and she became a *shawafa*."

After the reading, Zahara told David that he must come back again to remove the spell. She said the reading was the equivalent of fifty cents. I offered her $2. She scoffed at the idea of a tip.

"If you are so rich, why don't you take bread to the poor at the Shrine of Moulay Idriss?"

She then advised that I should never go to that sacred place without taking bread to the poor and buying ritual candles at the nearby candle *souk*.

Years later, Louise later told me what the *shawafa* told her in private; Zahara said that we would get married and have children. That prediction turned out to be only half accurate. We did get married, but we never had children.

From our limited observations, it would seem that Zahara was much more skilled at knowing about things in the present or past – even at great distances – but less able to predict the future.

Of course, fortune telling and telepathy are controversial in numerous respects. Many people in the West, perhaps most, view psychic phenomenon as somewhere between a superstitious relic of pre-scientific times or an outright scam on the gullible. Many Christian fundamentalists however don't dismiss that some individuals can predict the future but generally believe fortune tellers have gained that ability through some sort of deal with the devil.

Many conservative Islamic scholars similarly believe that fortune tellers and magicians get their powers from evil *djinn* who find humans who are willing to worship *djinn* in return for special powers. This they argue violates religious teachings in two respects; the faithful must worship none but God, and only God truly knows the future. Some conservative Muslims feel so strongly about this that in Saudi Arabia, fortune telling is punishable by death. At least at the time we lived in Saudi Arabia, Chinese restaurants were not allowed to give customers fortune cookies.

By contrast, Morocco has generally taken a much more liberal attitude on this and other matters of religious doctrine. That is usually attributed to Morocco's closer ties to Africa and its animistic practices. In Morocco it is not uncommon to see shops that combine herbalism and what might be described as folk medicine or witchcraft. It is on this account that the Saudis are so fearful of the powers of Moroccan women that they enacted laws forbidding Moroccan women from working as maids in Saudi homes, fearing that the Moroccan women might break up marriages by casting powerful spells.

Of course some humans are willing to corrupt every tool, capability or institution known to man. But that also necessarily implies that there are good people who will employ every tool, capability or institution known to man for the good. My sense was that Zahara fit into the latter category.

Shrine of a Sufi Holy man

Herbs and potions shop - Fez

12 - MEKNES

Our export plan was taking longer than expected to launch and we were going through our startup money despite our efforts to keep costs down by living on a shoestring. We thought that teaching English in the evening might bring in just enough extra cash without getting seriously in the way.

Although the Cultural Center was closed, the American Language Center was continuing to operate as a for profit entity run out of USIS Rabat. I called Rabat and talked to the woman who was the director of the program and asked if she needed an experienced hand. She said what she really needed was someone to be the Director at the Language Center in Meknes, which was going through some financial ups and downs.

Since Meknes was only fifty miles from Fez, I concluded that I could keep in touch with Naima and let things progress a little more slowly on the business front while ensuring our longer-term viability, so I took the offer. This also meant Louise could teach and we would have considerably more financial stability and our partners were thrilled that we didn't need to dig into the company coffers while doing the buying and shipping.

Our students were a mixed lot. Many were high school students who were using the evening classes to augment their English instruction in school by studying with native speakers. We also had quite a few Europeans who also wanted to improve their English, as well as to meet people and get out in the evenings in a city that didn't have too much evening entertainment. And finally, we had a significant number of pilots from the airbase just outside of town. Their tuition was paid by the Air Force, as English fluency was a prerequisite before they could go to the U.S. for advanced flight training.

The Language Center was in a quite pleasant, converted villa in the *Ville Nouvelle*. We had four classrooms, a kitchen and a wonderful, tiled courtyard with lemon trees. At night Louise and I stayed in our van at the local campground, but we kept clothing and took our meals at the Center. The caretaker of the Center was a friendly gentleman by the name of Driss. His wife did our cooking, and our life was well organized.

Driss was pushing seventy and said he was a veteran of the 'war in China.' I didn't know that Morocco had ever been in a war with China, and I pressed for more information.

"Oh yes, Mr. Bill, that was back in the early 50's, I was stationed in Saigon," he said confidently. He added that the French government still paid him a pension.

Now things made sense. Driss was referring to the Indochina War. Like the Brits, the French often recruited fighters from the colonies. Apparently, many Moroccans had served in Viet Nam, just as many Senegalese fought for the French when the Moroccans were fighting for independence.

Louise and I would often take cappuccino breaks at one of the nearby outdoor cafes, and one day along came 'Madame Clown.' This time 'Madame Clown' was wearing a bright yellow vinyl coat and yellow bonnet, and the same caked on bright red rouge as before.

I tried to get her to speak Arabic, but she looked at me like I had lost mind. Finally, I asked a Moroccan guy at the next table if he wouldn't mind translating from French to Arabic. This had her really baffled but she proceeded.

"She says that you are about to have an important meeting with an important military commander. She says you'd better go now, or you'll be late," the translator explained.

I asked, "Late for what?" and the translator repeated my question to her.

For the first time she became somewhat animated. She looked in my face like I was an idiot and shouted, "*Le rendezvous, le rendezvous!*"

I signaled the translator with my hand that no translation was necessary. I gave her some money and thanked them both as Louise and I headed off to the Center just a few blocks away.

"What do you think that was all about?" Louise wanted to know.

"I have no idea," I mumbled.

However, we weren't left in suspense for long. As we turned the corner, we noticed a black Mercedes with a military driver leaning against the car and looking at his watch.

As we approached, he asked, "Monsieur Keenan?"

I said yes in Arabic, trying to dispel him quickly of the notion that we were going to converse in French.

"You must come with me at once. The Commander is waiting. Madame will stay here," he instructed.

I was somewhat reluctant to just jump in this car and take off. I didn't know what was going on and I was more than a little bewildered about 'Madame Clown's prediction. Thoughts were racing through my mind.

"Are the clown and the Commander in cahoots?"

"Have I said something careless and they're going to throw me in the dungeon?"

"Do they mistakenly think I am a spy?" Nothing added up.

Finally, I asked the driver who this Commander was. He also looked at me like I was an idiot.

"The Commander of the airbase," he responded, "Who else?"

Well at least that was one piece to the puzzle. I decided not to embarrass myself further with more stupid questions. I concentrated on the lovely countryside leading out to the base. We soon passed through the security gates. The guards saluted and looked surprised to see me sitting in the back seat instead of the Commander. I have an appreciation for the 'theater of the absurd' and this was starting to qualify."

I was whisked into the Commander's office and was greeted warmly and asked whether I wanted coffee or tea. The Commander was a friendly, handsome man. He spoke English very well and got right to the point.

"Mr. Keenan, we have many of our pilots studying at the American Language Center and I am hoping that we might be able to tailor their studies more to their military professions," he said.

I felt a great burden leave my shoulders. Whatever the problems to be worked out around the English classes, it was becoming clear that no one was suggesting that I had behaved in any way that might harm Morocco's national security.

I began to explain, "I appreciate your concern, Commander. Of course, I must remind you that your pilots are in class with the general public. We can't start asking high school students and housewives questions about the finer art of high-altitude bombing. Nonetheless, the instructors have some flexibility, and they could direct different questions to the pilots, as long as it wasn't anything that would make non-military people uncomfortable. Also, we can give the pilots some special attention with homework which we would gladly take the extra time to review."

This all seemed reasonable to the Commander. But he had one more matter on his mind, "Mr. Keenan, I would also like you to communicate to the American Ambassador my disappointment that the F-5's that we were promised still haven't been delivered."

"Whoa boy," I was thinking to myself, "This guy is either dreaming or pulling my leg."

I proceeded carefully, "Sir, I will of course do what I can, but you must understand that given my position I really don't have access to the Ambassador."

"But surely you can pass a message through your supervisor that will get to the Ambassador, can't you?" he persisted.

I reluctantly agreed to pursue the matter. With that settled I finished my coffee and answered a few pleasantries about where I was from, and he talked about his own flight training in Texas. Then I was whisked back to the Center. On the way, I pondered what had just transpired. Was he just looking for an American to talk to, to impress? Perhaps he was really trying to pressure or embarrass the Ambassador by sending the message through back channels and low-level personnel.

In any case, the truly interesting question was how did 'Madame Clown' know about the meeting? When we saw her, she was coming from the opposite direction as the Center. It was unlikely that she had passed the Center and seen the driver waiting. Was she working with military intelligence or truly clairvoyant?

Several weeks later, we were at a gathering at the apartment of a couple who were with the Peace Corps. Of the ten people there, Louise and I were the only ones not in the Peace Corps, but our low incomes and naivete made us fit in perfectly. After a bit, someone asked if we ever had a reading from the old French lady. I asked if she meant the clown and she said yes and mentioned that she knew a little about her.

She said that 'Madame Clown's husband had been a high-ranking officer in the French military during the colonial period. After independence, her husband returned to France, but she stayed behind in Meknes. I wondered to myself if she had fallen in love with Morocco, or perhaps fallen in love with a Moroccan. In any case, she apparently had supported herself for a couple of decades walking up and down the boulevard giving tarot readings. Everyone at the gathering had stories of some amazing prediction that she made. There was speculation that she might be involved with the secret police, which might explain why she always seemed to have the inside track on things.

Then there was a knock at the door. I was nearest the door and assumed it was yet someone else coming to the little party. I opened the door. To the complete shock of everyone in the room, the little French clown/spy/clairvoyant/whatever was standing in the doorway with her patented dead pan expression.

"Did you call?" she asked.

We were all stunned. No one responded. We just looked at her with our mouths open.

After a moment, she said, "If you didn't have any questions, why did you call?"

We still had nothing to say. So, she wheeled around and left. I shut the door. One of the ladies laughed and said, "Oh my God, do you believe that?" In fact, I was still having a hard time believing it, my mind raced for a rational explanation. Had somebody at the party arranged for her to come? Perhaps the room was bugged, and this was an elaborate mind game by the Moroccan authorities? Perhaps. But given her reputation for the unexplainable, it was becoming more and more difficult to invent rationalizations.

That fall we took another grand tour of the country. Our friends Kip and Susan had just returned to Oregon from India and were game to give Morocco a try. They were particularly interested in experiencing Morocco's abundant natural beauty, so they arrived with camping gear. First stop was my favorite fishing lake in the Middle Atlas Mountains southeast of Fez, where my friend Grant had poached trout out of the King's fenced off private reserve.

We got to the lake in the afternoon and by all appearances we had the lake to ourselves, or so we thought. Kip and Susan quickly set up their tent. Louise and I stayed in the van as usual. The mountain air was invigorating, the sky was clear, and you felt like you could reach out and touch the stars. Then around nine, we heard some drums, chanting and singing from across the lake. We speculated that perhaps they were boy scouts. Whoever they were, the party went late, and I was getting a lot kidding from our guests about the 'quiet' lake I had promised.

We got up early and Susan made coffee and we joined them in the tent for breakfast. We were chatting about our plans for the day when the tent flap suddenly flew open, and four soldiers were pointing assault weapons in our faces. Needless to say, it was one of the more terrifying moments that we experienced during our time in Morocco.

We were still gasping for air when one of them said, "The King will be here shortly. You have to leave. You have ten minutes.

I said, "Believe me, we'll be out of here in five minutes."

As we were driving away green army personnel carriers started arriving and every fifty yards a soldier would pop out and scurry behind the bushes and trees along the road. Once we were safely back on the main road, we were finally able to catch our breath and started laughing about our memorable run in with the all the King's men.

Kip asked sarcastically if I had any more recommendations for 'quiet places' to camp.

"Not really, that was my best shot. We might as well head straight to Marrakesh and hang out with snake charmers and Gnawa musicians."

After several days in Marrakesh, we made our way up the Atlantic coast. We stayed overnight in Casa and went to a French restaurant for the world's most expensive ordinary pizza, which further undermined my reputation as a travel guide.

Fortunately, we had an open invitation to stay with Abdesalam and Rochma in Oued Laou and I was determined to make good on some of my promises. Thankfully, our time in Oued Laou was as blissful as ever and Kip and Susan got to experience living with a Moroccan family while having a 'quiet' Mediterranean beach holiday.

However, I must admit I was a bit nervous that the King's special forces were going to pop out of the surf at any moment.

It was almost time for Abdesalam and Rochma to head back to Fez, so they decided to leave earlier than planned so we could all go back through Chaouen and stay at Abdesalam's father's place.

After a few days of visiting Morocco's most beautiful city, we dropped off Kip and Susan at a seaside resort just south of Tangier where they could rest up in luxury before catching a plane back to Oregon.

As September turned into October, Louise and I decided on a whim to get out of Meknes for a day trip up into the Middle Atlas Mountains around Khenifra. There was very little traffic and we drove slowly, pulling over at especially scenic spots, of which the Middle Atlas has many. That also meant that it was dark while we headed back down the mountains. As we neared a village, we started hearing a lot of yelling and screaming. We weren't sure what to make of it. I was concerned that there might be some kind of protest going on, as there had been unrest in the area in recent times.

We approached the village cautiously, occasionally stopping to see if we could tell what the ruckus was all about. We really had no choice but to keep driving, so we pushed on. As we came into the village, we saw a large, noisy crowd out front of a café that had a TV propped up on a tall platform. As it turned out, the crowd was cheering for the boxers Muhammad Ali and Joe Frasier who were fighting it out in the legendary 'Manila Thrilla.' The Moroccans were of course cheering for Muhammad Ali who was a folk hero throughout the Muslim World.

Six years later we were living in Portland and Louise had an opportunity to meet Muhammad Ali when he was visiting her workplace. Louise told Muhammad about the adoring crowd surrounding the television in the mountains of Morocco. Muhammad loved the story and asked Louise if she knew any Arabic.

She responded with, "*salam alaikum warahmatullahi wabarakatuh*" (May the peace, blessings and mercy of Allah be with you.)

Muhammad's eyes opened wide, and he said, "My God, I am a Muslim, and this little white girl knows more Arabic than I do."

Then he told his brother to go out to the car and get a Prayer Book which he autographed for Louise.

In mid-October, Bob and Christie Newland arrived from Oregon for their part business, part pleasure tour of the country. After they recovered from the flight, we set out on our third whirlwind tour of the Morocco in five months. This time we spent more time up in the mountains, going from village to village looking for Amazigh flatweaves (known as kilims in the West and as *hanbals* in Morocco.)

One day we visited a weekly *souk* (market.) It was rather like an outdoor flea market. There were carpets, household goods, traditional breads and pastries, and piles and piles of fresh fruit and vegetables. We arrived at dawn and watched the locals come in on donkeys and carts with their wares. I spotted an old woman on a donkey hauling a fantastic old flatweave. It was faded blue and purple with white cross-stitching. It was about five by eight feet and had one badly worn spot the size of an orange, but the warp was still there. I knew that I could unravel yarn from one of the ends and do an invisible mending that no one but me or weaver would ever recognize.

I asked the old woman how much she was asking. She said the equivalent of $15. I offered her $12 and we settled for $13. Christie asked what had just transpired and I told her.

"You're sick," she said in disgust.

"Well, Christie, I don't want her to lose face, I have to bargain," I tried to explain.

"You heard me, SICK," she said doubling down on her diagnosis.

Christie then slipped the lady another twenty bucks with a wink. The lady was confused but happy to take the money. Of course, it was still robbery and Christie had succeeded in making me feel guilty. I knew that I had long ago begun to filter out much of my sympathies for Morocco's poor. In many ways it was the only way to cope. During my first few months in Morocco, I was handing money out to every beggar in town. It was a bottomless pit. Then they found out where I lived and were lined up at the door. You get to the point where you don't see it. You accept it as normal. You stop looking through your American eyes. You put limits on your charity.

Bob, however, gave the locals something better than money - entertainment. We were sitting in a restaurant and Bob suddenly jumped up and said, "Ladies and Gentlemen may I have your attention."

Of course, they had no idea of what he was talking about, but his body language suggested that it was showtime.

Moroccans are great storytellers, and the audience eagerly gave Bob their undivided attention. Christie began to laugh as she had seen the show before. I didn't know what exactly he was up to, but I had known

'Bobby' since the fourth grade, and this was perfectly in character - whatever it was.

Bob then pulled a long blonde hair from Christie's head, tied a noose at one end and showed it to everyone in the room. They would have been satisfied if that was the entire show. Then he began chasing flies around the restaurant, weaving deftly in and out between the tables. There is no shortage of flies anywhere in Morocco, but they are smaller and quicker than their American cousins. Still, it didn't take Bob long to snag one. (Remember the guy had been a wide receiver in the NFL) He then returned to our table and got the hair he had taken from Christie and slipped the noose over the fly's head and let the fly loose as he held one end of the hair. The fly flew in circles on its tether to the cheers of the amazed villagers. I suspect with his performance Bob did more for U.S. - Moroccan relations than the millions of dollars of American assistance.

The Newlands had been with us in Meknes for three weeks and intended to stay longer, however, the King unexpectedly announced the 'Green March.' His plan was to challenge Spanish control of the Sahara by sending 350,000 unarmed protestors across Morocco's southern border into the Spanish Sahara, forcing the King of Spain to either give up control or slaughter tens of thousands of unarmed Moroccans, all of whom were dressed in white and carrying green *Qur'ans*. It was a time of great tension and doubt about how things were going to play out. Travel to Marrakesh became restricted and we started to reconfigure our itinerary for the rest of the Newlands' stay. We decided to go to our favorite outdoor café on the boulevard, have some lunch and think it over. While we were eating, Christie spotted 'Madame Clown.'

"Is that the woman you told us about?"

I said, "Yeah, that's her alright. Let me grab her."

We cleared space at the table for 'Madame Clown' to spread out her playing cards.

She had only one thing to say, "Your guests are in great danger, and they must leave *tout de suite.*

I had already learned the futility of pressing Madame for more details than she was willing or able to provide. So, we decided it was time to drive the Newlands to Tangier where they would catch the ferry to Spain and begin their Eurail Pass tour of Europe.

When we returned to Meknes, the citizenry was quite riled up with local marches taking place daily in solidarity with those who volunteered to march into the Spanish Sahara. One afternoon a medium sized mob passed by the Language Center on their way to the boulevard to join a large march. When someone spotted the Netherlands plates on our van parked out in front of the Center, they started chanting slogans; then they began rocking the van back in forth and preparing to set it on fire. I wasn't sure why they thought the Netherlands had anything to do with the Spanish Sahara, but the crisis no doubt reignited long standing anti-European sentiments.

Louise and I decided to take cover and let the $500 van fend for itself. Then we heard someone yelling to the crowd to calm down and go away. There was some arguing, but the person told the crowd that the van was owned by his teacher, and it was shameful to treat a teacher of Moroccans in such a manner. We peered out and it was Hassan, one of our students. I opened a crack in the door to tell him to get inside, when I saw the crowd leaving.

I grabbed Hassan and pulled him inside. I thanked him, but also said, "We can get another car, but we can't get another you!" We were quite taken by his loyalty and bravery in single-handedly facing down an angry irrational mob. It spoke well for Morocco's chances of navigating the stormy seas ahead

Christie Newland in Berber silver necklace

MOROCCAN MYSTIQUE

Bob Newland at Volubilis Roman ruins

MOROCCAN MYSTIQUE

Kilims at Souk el Khemis

Christie and Louise with hand embroidered tablecloth

A palace gate - Meknes

Prayer book Muhammad Ali gave Louise

Close-up of Middle Atlas kilim

MOROCCAN MYSTIQUE

Abdesalam Ketami

Susan and Kip at Abdesalam's father's house in Chaouen

13 - FEZ APARTMENT

At the end of the fall term, I got a call from Rabat. I was told that Meknes Language Center's lease had not been renewed and it would be closed. I felt that students and I had been used. Clearly, officials in Rabat knew the status of the lease all along. On the other hand, I had gotten three months' salary and the students had another term of English that they otherwise would not have had. Anyway, I was happy to turn more of my attention to our export business.

We decided to move to Naima's mother's apartment full time as we had already collected a lot of merchandise and we wanted to wait until we had a full shipment before sending it to Oregon.

We also got some good news. The Fez American Cultural Center was reopening on a very scaled back basis and Louise got hired to classify, package, and ship the Center's fairly substantial library. This was all rather convenient. The apartment was on the same block as the Cultural Center. In years past, I often parked in front of the building while at work.

We were on the second floor and a very sweet couple with an adorable little girl occupied the adjoining apartment. They were close friends of Naima and the doors to our apartments were left wide open, as they had been when Naima's mother lived there. The wife would forever be bringing us different Moroccan dishes and pastries to try out.

The two apartments on the other side of the stairwell were far less harmonious. The respective wives in those apartments were both large ladies who looked a great deal alike but had very low opinions of each other. They would yell and wrestle in the hallway almost daily and it reminded me a good deal of Japanese *Sumo* wrestlers. Consequently, I reluctantly took on the responsibility of separating them and sending them to their apartments.

We came under attack ourselves late one night, not by the neighbor ladies, but by a mad man at the construction site adjacent our building. For some unknown reason the man decided to start heaving large cement blocks up onto the balcony of our apartment. I don't know if he was drunk, angry, didn't like Americans or had heard somehow that we had thousands of dollars of merchandise in the apartment that he might help himself to after he had chased us away. Whatever the case, he must have been incredibly strong as these were heavy cement blocks, and our apartment was on the second floor.

Our response was to simply roll down the shutters that most Moroccan buildings have, barricade the front door with boxes of merchandise and wait. After about twenty minutes of this aerial assault, we heard some yelling and the barrage halted. We cautiously emerged to find a huge pile of blocks on the balcony. The next morning, I asked the construction workers how their blocks got on my balcony. They said they were bewildered.

"Whatever the case, they are yours and you better remove them," I insisted.

Our other problems were less threatening. Thieves were forever breaking into our van. After they had taken my tools, they would break in just to sleep. I developed sensitive hearing and essentially slept with one eye open. One night I heard some noise on the street. I snuck out onto the balcony and could see a guy with his arm reaching through the wing window, feeling around for the door handle. As fate would have it, Louise had a row of very ripe tomatoes on the ledge of the balcony. I played a lot of sports in my day and was fairly confident in my passing accuracy. I grabbed a nice squishy tomato and fired it at the guy's head – bingo, splat, touchdown!

Then I quickly ducked behind some plants and didn't make a sound. He jerked back from the window and felt his head and then screamed "Allah" and took off running. I am not sure if he thought he had been shot and was bleeding or that *djinn* had intervened in his wrongdoing. I'd like to think that he was so spooked that he changed professions.

The other great entertainment from the balcony was watching 'Kiwi,' who was the famous town drunk, and possibly crazy as well. At night, he slept in the entrance to our building. He showered (with his clothes on) by standing under the drain spouts of the balconies, smiling, and singing, as though he had just won the New York Lottery.

Kiwi was once a wealthy businessman, but he gave away his money and took to living on the street. Across the street from the apartment, there was a high school, and since there was no air conditioning, the windows were usually open. There was a large cement ledge under the windows where Kiwi kept his *Playboy* magazines and bottles of Fanta mixed with wood alcohol. No one ever disturbed Kiwi's worldly possessions. Me, on the other hand, they tried to rob every night.

Kiwi would stand outside the classroom window at his ledge/bar, mix his drinks, comment on the class instruction, and show the students pertinent photos from *Playboy*. The photos seemed especially popular with the boys. No one ever told him to leave, shut up or otherwise interfere with his antics. I was very curious about all of this, but the Moroccans didn't really want to talk about it. They didn't seem embarrassed about it; they just weren't interested in letting me in on this aspect of their society.

I had already noticed that the Moroccans seemed to tolerate the more bizarre members of society more than Americans would. But Kiwi really seemed to be pushing the threshold. The rare times I saw him rebuked was after he started calling me '*haj.*' *Haj* is an honorific religious title reserved for someone who has made the pilgrimage to Mecca. Using the term *haj* for a *nazarani* (Christian) such as myself was no laughing matter. After Kiwi realized just how much this made everyone angry, he only relished the opportunity more. He began to take off his skull cap and bow every time he saw me.

"Peace be unto you, *haj*."

This put me in an uncomfortable position, and I always loudly proclaimed, "I am sorry, Sir, you are mistaken, I am not *a haj*."

"Oh, yes Sir, you are the most worthy *haj* of them all," he loudly proclaimed for all to hear. Now that would really infuriate them, which of course was his intent.

Religion is a sensitive issue in most countries and that is especially true in Muslim countries. Morocco is at the more liberal end of the Islamic spectrum, but that is still pretty conservative. The first thing Moroccans want to know when they meet you is your religion. In my case, once I began to speak Arabic there was the assumption and subsequent disappointment, that I had converted to Islam. For Europeans, it was assumed that they were Christians. A lot of Moroccans were unsure about Americans with whom they had had much less contact than the French or Spanish, who had colonized Morocco. I was once asked if I was an American or a Christian. That had me scratching my head a bit. I guess the thinking was that Americans are some kind of free form pagans - an impression that Hollywood has done a lot to foster.

After I had been in Fez for only a short time, I was at a Moroccan home and there were a number of men gathered in the *majlis* (sitting room.) I was asked in Arabic if I was a Christian. At that point my Arabic was so weak that I answered to one of the English speakers and explained that although I was baptized and raised a Christian and generally agreed with Christian teachings, I nonetheless was disillusioned with organized religion and thought of myself as a citizen of the world and a friend of all religions.

"What did he say?" the old man asked the translator, puzzled by my long winded responce.

I knew enough Arabic to understand the translator's response, "Oh, he just said he is a Christian."

The exchange was very educational for me. For Muslims, the issue is are you one of us or are you one of them. They couldn't care less about any other philosophical subtleties. From then on, I always answered simply that I was a Christian. I came to accept that I would have to bear whatever baggage that entailed. Of course, a lot of that baggage goes back to the Crusades, the numerous wars between the Ottomans and Europeans, and then three Arab-Israeli wars, two of which the U.S. was deeply involved. Moroccans were also subjected to decades of French colonialism. It is not a history which builds much trust.

Despite all of this, I found the Moroccans generally willing to forgive and forget. Even during the 1973 Arab-Israeli War, we had only one minor incident in Fez involving an American. There was also an apparently attempted bombing at a musical event sponsored by the American Cultural Center in Casablanca. In that episode, the batteries that were to ignite the bomb were inserted backwards, which inclined us to believe that it was more of a statement than an actual attempted bombing.

My problems in Morocco usually had less to do with politics and more to do with petty crime. I've already described how I got mugged on my first day in the country. When we were living in Meknes, someone used a long pole to reach through the ironwork protecting an open window and managed to open a closet and pull out my only suit and several of Louise's dresses. We were quite impressed by the thief's tradecraft, but undoubtedly, he had lots of practice.

On another occasion, a thief stole some clothes that were drying on the line on the roof of our Fez apartment. My landlord was a judge, and he came up with the suspect in a couple of hours. I went down to the police station to sign the complaint but first I asked if I could talk to the suspect. The police didn't want me to see him, but I insisted that was the only way that I would sign the complaint.

The young suspect looked more like one of my poor students than an enterprising thief. I knew that there had been many students arrested at some recent demonstrations. I asked the young man if he stole my clothes.

"Do these look like your pants?" he said, pointing to his beat-up, worn-out pants.

"No," I said, "But you could have sold my pants for the money."

I looked him straight in the eye, "Yes or No, did you steal my clothes?"

"No Sir, I didn't."

His eyes were absent of the smoldering hatred that I had seen in many of the younger guys, and I simply hadn't convinced myself that he was my thief. I didn't sign the complaint and the judge was rather upset with me.

"I am sorry Mr. Mohamed, I just can't send a young man to jail over my pants, unless I am reasonably certain he is the thief. I just don't feel it in my heart."

Our next defeat at the hands of the thieves was in the Fez *medina*. We had just picked up a bundle of Moroccan *kaftans* (dresses) at a tailor who did work for us. We wanted to check out some carpets, so we ventured further into the *medina*. I had a small bag cross strapped over my shoulder allowing me to hold it firmly in my armpit while I carried the package of *kaftans*. Suddenly a passing mule ladened with grain came crashing down on us. At first, I just thought that the mule had slipped. Then as we were trying to crawl out from under the mule, I saw a little kid about eight running off with what seemed to be a wallet. I couldn't imagine that it was mine; but I looked at my shoulder bag and it had been slit open. I was under the impression that the boy hadn't just spontaneously taken advantage of an opportunity that presented itself. My guess was the boy and the mule driver had a well-rehearsed act that played out several times a day. On the way home I stopped by a police station and reported the incident. The cop at the desk said, "You were lucky. The day before an Italian guy required stitches after his chest got slit open when they missed his bag."

When I tell people these stories, many of them ask why I am nonetheless so positive about Morocco. First, before I leave the wrong impression, only something like 2% of tourists experience theft. I was there for four years and that clearly increased the likelihood that I would have some problems. You also have to put that in perspective to the much more violent crime that plagues American cities like New York and Miami. In any case, my lasting impressions of Morocco are the colorful people, the great cuisine, fantastic architecture, beautiful scenery, uplifting music, and remarkable crafts, which were well worth losing a couple of pairs of pants and a few hundred dollars.

Probably the strangest thing that happened at the apartment had to do with the small boiler that was in the living room. It was primarily used to heat water for the bath. One day smoke inexplicably started coming out of it and we were baffled as to why. At first, I thought that its piping might have been connected to another boiler in an apartment below ours. Then I realized that the smoke smelled of sandalwood. I asked our neighbor if she had any idea of what was possibly going on.

She said, "*wallahee*, (My God) I better get Naima, she can explain."

When Naima arrived, she was very apologetic saying, "In the past this has only happened when family were staying here, I don't know why she would appear while you are here. Perhaps it means she has accepted you as family."

I asked who 'she' was. Naima responded, "My mother of course, she still visits her apartment."

I have since read that Muslim theology doesn't recognize that the dead return as ghosts. *Djinn*, on the other hand, do supposedly appear as dead people. In any case, all of this is well above my pay grade. My purpose is to simply give the reader a sense of the degree to which Moroccans regard the paranormal as normal.

Fez *medina*

Tannery - Fez

14 - MOROCCAN WEDDINGS

Naima understood our keen interest in Moroccan culture, and she frequently combined our business trips in Casa with her family events. When her sister Rashida and her cousin Fuad planned back-to-back wedding receptions, we lined up appointments with some Casablanca clothing manufacturers. Then a couple of days before Rashida's reception, we loaded up the van with Naima and her two young boys and drove the normally three-and-a-half-hour trip to Casa. Unfortunately, the trip was made longer because the boys had never been for a long drive before and they kept getting car sick. Thankfully we arrived before dark, and I was able to take the boys for a short walk while the ladies prepared dinner.

The next morning, we were up early, and the van paid for itself on that day as we spent the whole day buying groceries and flowers, renting furniture, and taking Rashida to the *coiffure*. When I went back to pick up Rashida, I hardly recognized her as she looked more like Madame Butterfly - covered with silk and jeweled butterflies. Then when we got back to the apartment, I hardly recognized Louise, who had been transformed into a blonde Moroccan. Naima had dressed her in one of Rashida's gorgeous *kaftans* and draped her in gold jewelry. She was a Moroccan princess for a day.

Rashida's apartment had also been transformed. Small tables were set up around the apartment, circled with leather puffs to sit on. Rashida had a spacious apartment, but they were expecting eighty guests. Later that afternoon everything was ready to go, and we all took a much-welcomed break of mint tea and cookies.

Around seven, the band was the first to arrive. Relative to most bands, they didn't have that much equipment – midsized speakers, and a small set of traditional Moroccan *tabla* drums. Besides the drummer, there was a violinist, a flautist, and an *oud* player. (An *oud* is the pear-shaped stringed instrument that is a member of the lute family.) The flautist carefully set up a stand with his various bamboo and wooden flutes. Meanwhile the violinist unpacked his case and connected an electrical cord between his violin and the speakers. This was the first time I had seen an electrified violin and I was more than curious about what to expect. He then gently positioned the violin on a stand, went over to his bag and pulled out a bottle of Jack Daniels which he set on the floor in front of the violin. Given that alcohol was illegal in Morocco, I thought his open defiance was rather bold. I looked at Naima and raised my eyebrows. She laughed and explained to us that the gentleman frequently appeared on television and was very famous; we were exceedingly lucky to have him at the reception, whatever his requirements. Rashida's husband Abdulatif was a very successful photographer, and it was only because of his excellent connections in the television and music community that he landed such a famous musician for the reception.

A half hour later the guests began to arrive, and the room quickly came alive. The guests were speaking a mix of Moroccan Arabic and French, but mostly French as the Moroccan education system was taught exclusively in French until 1972, and the Casablanca elite gravitated toward French culture, without totally abandoning their Moroccan roots. The ladies were all wearing elegant *kaftans* overlaid by sleeveless, transparent *dfinas* made from Indian silk saris with gold filagree. All of which was gathered at the waist by two to three inch wide, intricately carved gold wedding belts. Naima said the dresses were locally tailored for a minimum of $500. The gold wedding belts cost $1,000 and up (1976 prices). Most of the dresses were black, which really popped out the gold in a most stunning manner. The men were dressed in expensive French suits, and the atmosphere was that of a Los Angeles cocktail party, save for the fact no alcohol was available – unless you played violin.

The minute the band started I knew I was about to experience a night that would permanently alter my taste in music. The violin was utterly divine, and the *oud* and flute made their own statements about what paradise might sound like.

Of course, Moroccan music is greatly influenced by Middle Eastern music. Nonetheless, Andalusian music is uniquely Moroccan, and we were witnessing its early migration to electrified Andalusian. Fifty years later we are seeing this music becoming hugely popular in the West under the genre of Oriental Deep House.

What impressed me as much as the music was the elegant dancing of the ladies in their gorgeous *kaftans*. When we talk about Moroccan dancing, most people think of scantily dressed belly dancers gyrating around a restaurant. It is not that some of the belly dancers aren't quite amazing, but the gently swaying ladies at the wedding were far more exotic. Watching them, I came to realize a good dancer leads with her (or his) hands. Graceful hands, leading graceful wrists and arms, then the hips and legs have no choice but to join the party. My friends the Funkadelics once recorded an album called *Free Your Mind, Your Ass Will Follow*. The Moroccan equivalent would be *Free Your Hands, Your Hips Will Follow*.

This lesson was enormously useful to me years later when I began my recovery from a severe case of rheumatoid arthritis. I woke one morning nearly paralyzed. I couldn't get out of bed. I had frozen shoulders, and my left knee wouldn't bend. I had Louise do a Google search for "yoga AND frozen shoulders." We came up with a YouTube video of a yoga instructor who said, "Whatever you do, do NOT do yoga; you will rip yourself apart. Start by twirling a finger. If that feels O.K., try two fingers. The body loves pleasure and movement is pleasurable, as long as you don't overdo it. After a few days, start rotating your wrist. Soon enough your shoulders will loosen."

I followed his instructions and remembered the elegant hand movements of the wedding dancers in Casablanca. I mimicked the graceful movements of their fingers and hands. At first, I was a bit embarrassed as it seemed quite effete. However, it felt wonderful, and I realized I had to make a choice between incredible pain or not worrying about what other people thought.

As I began to recover, I was able to add one more element of Moroccan dance to my exercise routine. Moroccan Sufi and Gnawa dancers are men (and women) who do what you might describe as tribal line dancing. They move in unison, chanting to the rhythm of traditional percussion instruments. Much like the whirling dervishes, they absorb themselves in the repetitive movements until reaching a trance-like state which elevates their minds from their bodies. Of course, any of kind gentle rotation of the joints reduces inflammation and keeps joints healthy; dance is also very aerobic. Generally speaking, the traditional Moroccan lifestyle embodies many healthy practices - with the notable exception of their overly sweetened tea.

The very next day Naima's cousin Fuad also had a wedding reception with his new bride. The two wedding receptions were scheduled back-to-back to accommodate all the family that would be coming from Fez to Casablanca for both celebrations.

Fuad's father was a wealthy Fez businessman, and Fuad was marrying the daughter of one of his father's even wealthier Casablanca business associates. It was love, with the added benefit of a business merger.

The celebration started with a procession from the groom's home to the bride's palatial residence. Louise and I led the procession because our van was jam packed with gifts for the bride – everything from a huge cake, gold rings and bracelets, dresses, perfume, incense, henna, and last but not least, the traditional Moroccan wedding gift of huge cones of sugar. Somehow, we also managed to get two traditionally dressed Amazigh women in the van. Their job was to loudly chant *Qur'an* the entire way to the bride's home. We never fully ascertained the significance of their role, but we assumed it had something to do with purifying the gifts and protecting the bride from spells or possession by *djinn*.

When we arrived at the residence, several maids came out and unloaded the van and carted off the cake and all the gifts. We were then led into a grand salon, where three hundred guests were beginning to assemble. We were seated at a table where Naima, her sister and three cousins were sitting. After all the guests were seated, a grand procession entered the hall with the bride raised high on a flower covered *palanquin* that her escorts carried on rails, swaying back and forth to the rhythms of the drums and horns. Once at the front of the hall she was transferred to a *dais* where the groom joined her. The bride was so weighed down with gold that I suggested to Louise that they must have been worried that she was going to try to get away. After the ceremony was over, food started pouring out of the kitchen and just kept coming - roasted lamb, followed by honey marinated chicken, then a *tajine, basteeyah* (pigeon pie), more fresh salads, and when you couldn't eat any more, it was time for baklava, mint tea, and Turkish coffee.

The wedding excitement was so infectious that the groom's father spontaneously announced that he decided to marry a younger second wife. His decision, however, was not well received, especially by the women in his extended family. Louise and I were sitting at a table near where the groom's father was seated and we noticed an abrupt reduction in the service at his table. Nor did his plaintive appeals for assistance catch anyone's attention. We were all eating like royalty and the father was having a hard time getting coffee. This scenario went on all evening and after several hours the father announced that upon further reflection, he would rather get a new car than a second wife. Miraculously food suddenly began to appear at his table.

The music on the first night of Fuad's reception was provided by an excellent Andalusian band, although ironically it was not as magical as the Andalusian band at Rashida's far more humble party the night before. Nonetheless, at Fuad's party we witnessed a woman who danced herself into a trance, fell to the floor in what looked like an epileptic fit, before other guests carefully bundled her up and carried her off to a side room to recover. No one seemed surprised or concerned, and we had the definite impression that this was not all that unusual. I was aware that sort of thing was fairly common in more rural Sufi and Gnawa settings, but it seemed rather incongruous at this glitzy Casa high society event – another reminder that Morocco maintained its traditional character even as it painted on a new face for the global economy.

The following day there was a wedding party for the younger crowd. This time things were more casual and the atmosphere was more French than Moroccan. The music was by a local rock group playing mostly famous American cover tunes, which were nicely done. The women were wearing the latest Parisian designer casual fashions, and the men were wearing sports coats without ties. Again, the food was fabulous and abundant, and the dancing continued late into the early morning.

On the return trip to Fez, Naima asked us when we were getting married. We said we would have to wait a bit. For one thing, the Moroccan authorities wouldn't marry non-Muslims, so we would have to go to Gibraltar, and we were extremely busy trying to get our first big shipment ready to go. We decided to wait until the shipment was safely on its way. Then we ran into delays with Moroccan customs because I initially refused to pay *baksheesh* (under the table fee) to customs. I eventually realized they weren't going to budge. I paid up and the shipment flew off.

With the shipment on its way, Louise and I made our way to Gibraltar where the British were willing to marry us. It was a straightforward civil ceremony before a British magistrate, except for the fact that Louise had to first sign an affidavit attesting that she was still a 'spinster.' Louise asked if this was a joke and the magistrate laughed and explained that in British legalese spinster simply meant single. I didn't want to open another can of worms by asking why they didn't care if I was single.

I flubbed my vows a bit by saying "I take you for my life," instead of for "my wife."

The magistrate laughed and said, "Not to worry, in fact that is even better." Then he told Louise that he was her witness to what I had vowed.

After that, it was a four-day honeymoon of Indian curries and fish and chips. Gibraltar is a pleasant place, but quite small and it certainly doesn't take four days to see everything. Regardless, it was a nice change of pace from Morocco, and we returned to Fez refreshed and ready to get back to work.

However, Naima was adamant that we were regarded as family and consequently had to have a proper Moroccan wedding reception in Casablanca with her family. Rashida said that we worked so hard to help with her reception that she wanted to host our reception at her place. Only a fool would turn down a Moroccan party, and we agreed.

Once again, the ladies decked Louise out in a lovely *kaftan* with a gold wedding belt and tons of jewelry, accented by her long natural blonde hair. She was a very stunning Moroccan bride. Rashida prepared a fabulous feast, and we danced to recordings of our new favorite violinist who had impressed us so much at Rashida's reception.

Since we were already in Casablanca, we decided we would make another trip to the *shawafa*. Zahara repeated the rituals as before and slipped into her apparent trance. This time she wanted to talk about my family.

She said I had sister who had someone other than her family living with her, and this sister had just acquired a large piece of land and all of them were doing well. However, there was bad news; my father had health problems. Regardless, she said not to worry; he would live many more years. I would nonetheless have to return home to my family. She said that I would eventually return to Morocco, as I would come to Morocco three times.

I later asked Naima about this because I had already come to Morocco twice, but I had been in and out Morocco on day trips to the Spanish enclaves every six months to avoid the import tax on the van. Naima said that Zahara seemed to use the number three metaphorically, meaning several. In any case, Zahara was very clear that I would return.

I have two sisters. The older one, Jean, was my business partner. My other sister Kathryn's son Shan was adopted. The fact that he was adopted was fairly obvious as he is African American, and his siblings, Kelly, Kami and Jeff are Caucasian. This was well known to Naima, and pretty much everyone else in Fez, as my sister and her husband Steve spent a number of months in Morocco several years earlier, and everywhere their family went there was a big commotion as the Moroccans assumed that Shan was Moroccan, and he must have been kidnapped by these Americans. Naima could have passed this information on to the *shawafa*, although that was quite unlikely. In any case, even I hadn't heard anything about Kathryn buying a large property, or any problems with our father's health.

After the session, Zahara asked a favor. She didn't have a car and she would like to visit a nearby *marabout*, which is the tomb of saint. Moroccans often visit the shrine of a saint to receive blessings or to ask for help with a problem. The shrine where we took Zahara was on the Atlantic coast just south of Casablanca. When we got there Naima and Zahara went inside while Louise and I waited. The *marabout* itself seemed a bit run down but its location overlooking the ocean was quite beautiful.

The excursion was also an opportunity to get to know Zahara outside of her role as a *shawafa*. I couldn't help but wonder if she really was possessed by a *djinn*, or if that only occurred while she was in a trance. By all appearances she was a very humble and devoted young mother of very modest means. I have since read accounts about other Moroccan *shawafas* who were fabulously wealthy, with plush offices and wealthy international clienteles. By contrast, Zahara once refused my offer of a two-dollar tip and this short ride to the *marabout* was the only favor she ever asked.

Naima had once recounted a story how after the King's plane had been attacked, he supposedly sent a representative to see Zahara and she instructed the King that a powerful curse had been cast on his plane and he would have to bury his plane deep in the ground, which he allegedly did. Other than the fact that I knew Zahara had no interest in money, it didn't quite add up that a woman living in a shanty town would have a king for a client. One time I heard her talking to Naima and she kept referring to garbage, I told Naima that I didn't understand what she was talking about. Naima laughed and said that Zahara always called money garbage. It was rather apparent to me that had she wanted, Zahara could have had a wealthy clientele and become rich, but she consciously chose to stay among her people - the poor and oppressed Amazigh.

When we got back to Rashida's house, I called my sister Kathryn.

"Your ears must have been burning," she said, "I been trying to call you. You know, Dad has been diagnosed with colon cancer. We still aren't sure just how serious it is, but Mom is a nervous wreck. This is not a good time for you to be thousands of miles away. We need you here."

There was no question but that we would return. But I had one other thing on my mind, "Did you buy some property?"

"Yeah, we bought seventeen acres of gorgeous forested land outside of Wilsonville. I can't wait to show you. Who told you, we just got it?"

"Oh, a lady here in Casablanca. It's a long story. I'll tell you all about it when we get back to Portland," I said.

"Sounds interesting," she said.

"Very interesting," I replied.

Louise, Naima, and I quickly returned to Fez. Then we packed our bags for the return trip to Casa. I was reluctant to leave. I was confident that Naima could handle things at the Moroccan end, but it still upset our business plan and the matter of us returning to Morocco seemed questionable.

A few days later we were making goodbye hugs at the Casablanca International Airport. We caught a Pan Am flight that went through Lisbon. Not long after we took off, the stewardesses started passing out ham sandwiches. Of course, Muslims don't eat pork and the Moroccans on the plane were outraged at what appeared to be an intentional offense by Pan Am. As soon as the stewardesses turned their backs, the passengers started pelting them with ham sandwiches. Not too long after that Pan Am declared bankruptcy, prompting Louise to comment, "Well, I can count about 120 Moroccan spells that Pan Am had on their corporate heads."

Amazigh wedding procession -Azrou

MOROCCAN MYSTIQUE

Badrazeen, Hafiz, Louise, and Naima

Couscous and *tajine*

15 - FATE DISGUISED AS A RAFFLE

Soon after our return to Portland we learned that my father could be treated without surgery, and he lived another twelve years. Unfortunately, our Moroccan carpet and craft shop did not do as well. We had lovely things, but we weren't experienced marketing people. Eventually, we closed the store. I tried to keep it going on the wholesale end by working as a security guard at night so I could make sales calls by day, but it wasn't happening. Interior designers loved the Moroccan carpets and kilims, but it takes a while to catch on and we just weren't prepared for the long haul. I had to get a real job.

My mother passed away in 1986 and my father two years later. I was glad that I had those years with them. My experiences in Morocco faded but never disappeared. When my father passed away, he left me money to continue my education. We lived in Portland, and Portland State University had one of the few Arabic programs in the United States. I combined my Arabic and Middle East studies with my interest in the then immerging multimedia field and got an interdisciplinary master's degree.

Before I graduated, I was offered a contract at King Fahd University of Petroleum and Minerals in Dhahran, Saudi Arabia. I taught English and helped with their computer language learning program. It was a nice environment, but I was tempted by the higher salaries outside the academic community. After two years at the university, I switched over to an American contractor working for a Saudi ministry. I worked in graphic design and the development of computer-based training. Louise got a job as an English editor with the Ministry of Finance, and it wasn't long before our own finances were looking much better.

Louise and I continued to travel but we wanted to take advantage of places nearby and to see some new territory – like Turkey, Syria, Jordan, Bahrain, Qatar, and the UAE. We also made several trips to the Greek Islands. We always talked about returning to Morocco, but it was unreasonably expensive from Saudi Arabia. For just one of us it was around $1500 when we could go to Greece for $600. So, we put it off and talked about going to Gibraltar for our 25th Wedding Anniversary and taking the ferry to Tangier and retracing some steps.

One day while we were in Santorini another business venture jumped into our minds. Why not build a travel website and use our vacations to get it up and running? The name Top10GreekIslands.com came to mind. We checked to see if the domain had been taken; surprisingly, it was still available. We also registered the domains MoroccoTop10 and TravelTop10, but we decided it would make more sense to focus on the Greek Islands, and leave Morocco for another time, *Insha'Allah* (God Willing.)

We made several more trips to different Greek Islands and put together what turned out to be a rather successful travel site. In those early days of the internet there were only a handful of other sites on the Greek Islands, and we quickly moved to the top ranking. The income from the website was starting to offset some of our travel expenses, nonetheless our Greek adventures had burned through a fair amount of our savings, and we decided we would have to put off a trip to Morocco for some time to come.

One day a Moroccan lady who worked with Louise at the Finance Ministry, mentioned the annual bazaar at the Moroccan Ambassador's residence. We had been unaware of this event and were eager to check it out.

The minute we entered the walls of the residence it felt as if we had been teleported to Morocco. There was the undeniable beat of Gnawa music, the sweet violins of Andalusian music, the fragrant smell of sandalwood, mint tea, *tajines* and *basteeyah* (pigeon pie.) We frequently visited Western communities behind closed gates in Riyadh, but this was our first adventure into a 'little Morocco.' A fair number of professional Moroccans find their way to Saudi Arabia, where their skills are considerably more lucrative than at home. Nonetheless, most Moroccan expats preferred the more open environment of the other Gulf States, consequently, the Moroccan population in Riyadh was comparatively small.

We soaked up the sun and the music. While we were feasting on a delicious Moroccan lamb *tajine*, we heard a public announcement that the raffle on an airline ticket to Casablanca would be closing soon. What the heck I thought, $5 and I was feeling lucky. This little taste of nostalgia was quite powerful. Although I had never won anything of consequence before, I began to sense this was my turn.

The man selling tickets was a Royal Air Maroc agent. I handed him my money and told him, "This time I am going to win, I can feel it!" He laughed, "Well, that's good, confidence helps." He said the drawing would be held at midnight, but I didn't have to be there in person; they would call the winner. He said I just needed to put my phone number on the back of the ticket.

We went home and around ten went to bed. We didn't hear the phone during the night, and I woke up rather disappointed; I had fooled myself with great expectations. Nonetheless, I checked the message machine just to be sure and indeed there was a message. We slept through the call. With great expectation I played the message.

"Hello, Mr. Keenan, this is Marofi at Royal Air Maroc, it is my pleasure to congratulate you on …………brrrrrrkkkkkkkkkkkkkkkkkkkk…sssssssssssskkkkkkkkrrrrrssssssss."

He was holding the microphone too close to the phone and was picking up static. I couldn't hear the rest of the message.

I was devastated. I finally won something, something that I could almost touch, and I slept through the call. I was sure they must have moved on to another selection. I waited until I thought the Ambassador would be awake and drove back to the Ambassador's residence. The security guard was highly amused to see this panicky American speaking his Moroccan Arabic dialect. He called the Ambassador's wife. After a few moments she came out in her bathrobe smiling and told me to relax; the ticket was mine.

When I got home, Louise did a little dance, and we began to plan. She had already arranged to return to the States for a few months. She could fly through Paris and get a round trip ticket from Paris to Casablanca. Perfect.

I asked Louise, "Do you think the *shawafa* had a hand in this?"

Louise laughed, "It's more likely that the muggers pooled their money so they could get another crack at you."

Not only were we on our way, so was our Moroccan travel site. We decided that for the Moroccan site we would feature the top ten hotels. Morocco has stunning hotels with some of best examples of Moorish architecture in the world. Fortunately, our Top10GreekIslands was still rated number one in its category, so we were able to use it for credibility when making our proposals to the Moroccan hotels.

Our plan was to spend one night in the twenty different five-star hotels that we had selected and then put together a website rating the top ten. The remaining ten hotels would also get pages on the site but would not be rated. Not only would we get a chance to visit and photograph the best hotels in Morocco, but our rooms and dining would be provided by the hotels. After a flurry of faxes, the hotels agreed to the plan, and we established an airtight itinerary. Normally we preferred to travel at a much more relaxed pace but this time we were on a mission to see the best of Moroccan hotels and build a website that captured their splendor.

Our friends were surprised by our plans. Not only were we known to be strong proponents of taking slow-motion, low-key vacations, but we also had a long history of disparaging the tourism industry's creation of a commercialized 'derivative Morocco' as opposed to the 'real Morocco' that we cherished despite its rough spots.

Perhaps it was because we had come to appreciate what the Greek tourism industry had accomplished, that we started to see Moroccan tourism in a different light. For one thing it had become 30% of the Moroccan economy and was providing much needed income for Moroccan families. It was also providing an enormous investment in traditional Moorish architecture, crafts, and carpets, which meant that the craftsmen would have jobs and their superb skills wouldn't be forgotten. As the project came together, we became increasingly enthusiastic. We had already thoroughly experienced traditional Morocco, now it was time to get a better understanding how that was going to evolve in the modern global economy.

My previous trips to Morocco had been by ferry either from Gibraltar or Spain. This was the first time that I flew into Morocco and once again I was impressed by how green it was. I could see miles and miles of glittering strips of plastic wrap protecting ground crops. As the plane touched down, I thought back to the last time I had been to the Casablanca airport to pick up my parents in 1972. At that time the airport was little more than a runway and a sleepy café. When we got on the airport shuttle to our hotel it was hard not to notice that the driver was puffing on a hash pipe.

My mother asked, "What is he smoking? It smells weird."

I told her, "Mom it's probably best you don't think about it."

Undeterred she asked, "But will it be safe?"

"We can only hope," I sighed.

However, when I flew into Mohammed V International in 2000, the airport had become a huge modern facility with duty free shops and flights going in every possible direction. Louise's flight from Paris arrived a couple of hours after mine, so I had time to watch the airport 'people show' and reflect on how much Morocco had changed since we left. Fortunately, Louise's flight arrived on time, and we were on schedule to begin another Moroccan adventure. It is about a half-hour drive into the city center, and it was only $20 for a Mercedes taxi - quite reasonable by international standards and the driver was noticeably NOT smoking a hash pipe.

We drove through green rolling countryside with large estates and farms. We also passed a few shanty towns before coming upon Casa's new industrial zone with large factories and assembly plants of familiar multinational corporations. The inner city had gone in two directions. One was trendy new apartment buildings and sprawling homes. The other face was a sea of satellite dishes hovering over dilapidated tenements that hadn't seen a can of paint since the French left in 1956. New technology was also noticeable on the street as well. In 1976 it was very difficult to get a telephone line; in 2000 everyone was sporting a cell phone.

Finally, we pulled into the turnaround at the Royal Mansour Hotel. The sharply dressed, red uniformed bellhops descended on the shiny black Mercedes taxi. The front of the Mansour is graced by three tall amber colored arches with deeply etched Islamic designs. It is one of the most impressive hotel entries that you will see. We were ushered to the front desk, welcomed, and told that the sales manager would meet us after we had a chance to rest.

The hallways in the Mansour were decorated with carved Islamic designs and handmade mosaic tiles. It was the kind of architectural detailing one sees in many Moroccan hotels. It is hard to comprehend the amount of work and craftsmanship that went into a single hallway. This craft has developed over hundreds of years and has been used to adorn mosques and palaces throughout the Middle East. One of the most beautiful examples is the Al-Hambra in Granada, Spain, built by the Moors during their Andalusian conquest.

Morocco's finer hotels are an important part of the Moroccan experience. Not only will you see some of the better examples of Moorish architecture; you have a chance to live with it and soak up the incredible accomplishment of the craftsmanship and design. I was reminded of how a poster of Moroccan architecture in the window of a Gibraltar travel agency changed the direction of my life. Time and again I've been surprised at how much one's spirit can be lifted by a single arch or how much a single row of Moorish tiles can do to bring a room to a new level of grace and elegance. I have heard it said that is because the whole purpose of Islamic design is to inspire the faithful with a taste of Paradise. Not surprisingly the Goths borrowed from the Muslim architects to build their great cathedrals in Europe. If you have an ounce of architect or interior designer in your soul, you really must explore the world of Moorish architecture.

After all that praise of Moroccan interiors, I should mention that although the hallways at the Mansour are all intricately carved plaster, the rooms themselves are French baroque - lovely hardwood furniture and a large marble bathroom. It is all very tasteful but not very Moroccan. One might nonetheless argue it is appropriate for Casablanca, given that Casa is a Moroccan-French hybrid.

After we bathed, we got a call from Mohamed Mechuar - the hotel's sales manager and he dropped by the room. It had been twenty-four years since I had my meetings with the Casablanca exporters. Back then they always made me feel uncomfortable. They refused to believe that I didn't speak French and acted like I was putting them down as unsophisticated by speaking to them in Arabic. Mohamed was just the opposite. He insisted that I speak only Arabic with him even though he could have just have easily spoken to me in English (or French or Spanish for that matter), but he wasn't trying to impress me. He knew I had come for a Moroccan experience, and he wanted me to feel as though I was in his home.

Of course, I was not only there to look at the hotel and experience its services, but I also came to photograph. I had one camera with slides, and another with film, but I was planning to do most of the photography with a new digital camera as the photos were to be used principally on our website.

Digital cameras had just come out and no one in Morocco had ever seen one before. My camera was relatively small and had a transparent orange plastic case that showed all the inner working components. At first the hotel managers were exceedingly skeptical that it was a real camera and that I was a real photographer. That quickly changed when I instantly showed them the photos on their computer. My status immediately shifted from charlatan to magician – often causing the managers to upgrade our room.

One of the great advantages of being a photographer is that you have tremendous access to the facilities, an excuse to chat up all the staff and license to roll around on the floor behaving oddly.

As I visited the Royal Mansour's conference halls and saw the fashionable young Moroccans at the meetings and press conferences, I started to realize just how confident this generation was. By watching their football teams and runners lead the world, they started to see a new image of themselves; it was an image they hadn't seen since the Andalusian era – they wanted to be leaders not followers. It had been just three months since the passing of King Hassan II. Even the man with nine lives could not escape old age. After forty years of their love-hate relationship with the King, the Moroccans seemed mostly saddened by his death. He had taken them to better times and kept the country out of the worst of the crises that had cursed the rest of North Africa and the Middle East. We went to the beautiful new Hassan II Grand Mosque. Like the King, its construction was highly controversial. It had cost billions that the Moroccans could ill afford. Yet in the end it is not so much a monument to a king as to an era. As

I looked at the swarm of Japanese tourists staring up at the minaret in wonder, I realized that Casablanca now also had its own tourist destination along with the imperial cities Marrakesh, Fez, Rabat, and Meknes.

At the time we were there, the new King Mohamed VI, appeared to be inspiring respect and confidence. Of course, he was in that honeymoon period that new heads of state enjoy, but it was interesting to see pictures in Moroccan homes of the casually dressed young King. Perhaps it was just good PR, but he seemed to have convinced his country that, at least for now, he was one of them - young and ready to face the techno-global economy.

From Casa we flew the short but mountainous distance south to Agadir. We would have preferred to drive the pleasant but slower road along the coast, but we were on a very tight schedule – seventeen hotels in twenty days. The Moroccans thought we were nuts and of course we were. We generally travel much slower, but this time we had a mission - selecting Morocco's top ten hotels.

Agadir has a new and easy to negotiate airport. The large number of European charter aircraft lined up on the tarmac made it clear that it was no sleepy resort. The Europeans have been coming there in droves as soon as the city was rebuilt after the 1960 earthquake.

We finagled with several of the car rental companies and finally settled on a mid-sized Peugeot. We threw our luggage in the trunk and headed the ten miles into town. The city is visibly divided into the day-to-day Moroccan city and the beachfront European resort that stretches for twelve kilometers.

We spent the first night in the lovely Hotel Medina Al Salam. The hotel makes use of the *hareem* screen covered balconies that you would see in Old Jeddah, Saudi Arabia.

It had me wondering why Saudi hotels are such bland, modern

concrete nothings, and this hotel several thousands of miles away was so effectively using traditional Saudi architecture.

The Medina Al Salam has lush landscaping with more than generous use of bougainvillea. The swimming pool is large and sculptured. The shallow end is gradually sloped so that you can just walk in and out without a ladder and there is a small palm covered island in the center of the pool. It reminded me of a couple of the oases that we had camped in near Ouarzazate many years ago. That night we chose to indulge ourselves and feasted at the huge barbecue by the pool. Of course, we had just come from Riyadh in the middle of the Saudi Nadj desert and the pounding roar of the Atlantic carried us away to a restful night of sweet dreams.

Hotel Medina Al Salam is located just above the beach strip of restaurants, cafés, shops, and hotels. It is a short walk to the beach, but the beach is unusually wide, so the water is a bit distant. Consequently, there is absolutely no problem finding a place to throw your towel with an element of privacy. Of course, if you prefer, there are cafes with lounge chairs and hotels with their restaurants beachside.

Later that next day, we drove along the coast heading north up to Essaouira. It is not far before you pass the sprawling beach estate of the late Prince Sultan, who at the time was the

Saudi Minister of Defense Saudi Arabia. There were a couple of Moroccan gendarmes guarding the gates to his palace and, they apparently saw opportunity knocking as we drove by, and they waved us over.

"Did you know that you passed that bus?" they asked, peering into the windows.

"Yes, is there a problem? I said giving him my international driver's license.

"Of course you know it is illegal to pass buses?"

"No Sir, I didn't," I answered genuinely surprised. I suspected that he was scamming me, but I had long since learned the foolishness of getting into an argument with the gendarme.

"Where are you from? he asked."

I suddenly realized that I had a problem on my hand. I knew that these guards might take undue concern about this Saudi resident showing up at the palace of the Minister of Defense. I took a calculated risk. I told him that I was an English teacher from Fez on vacation. I said we had flown down and rented the car. Of course, if he inspected my international driver's license or my passport carefully, he would have known that I was a Saudi resident and then he would be really suspicious as to why I wasn't being truthful. I was in fact once an English teacher in Fez, and if necessary, I would claim that I had misunderstood his tenses.

"You know that is going to cost you 400 dirhams ($50) my friend," he said pulling out the ticket book and his pen.

I said, "Sir, I am on vacation, and I would really like to avoid going to court and spending hours standing in line. Maybe I could just give you 200 dirhams and be on my way. That would save us both trouble and I will have still learned my lesson about the buses."

"But I am afraid you might think I was a bad man for taking your money," he said cautiously moving toward a deal.

"Oh no, not so Sir, you would be doing a tourist to Agadir a big favor, I assure you it is just between the two of us." (Perhaps I should have said, it is just between you and I, and everyone else who reads this book.)

The following day we headed south through truck farming country for about 50 miles to Tiznit. Tiznit has a walled old *kasbah* that held some promise, but we were on a tight schedule up to a small mountain hotel in the region off to the east, toward Marrakesh. The Kerdous Hotel is a little terracotta colored castle with a white rim that is perched on a high mountain top. It has no apparent *cause de l'existence* other than a chance to escape the desert heat down below. The well paved road meanders through the rolling foothills, passing a few villages and a lovely palm tree river oasis, but it is mostly barren to the top.

The Kerdous has an unusually arabesque shaped pool overlooking the valley below. Inside, the hallways is a veritable museum of indigenous Moroccan oil paintings. The floors are covered with local Amazigh tribal carpets. The slightly florescent intricate designs on the doors overshot the mark a bit, but the overall atmosphere was quite authentic and refreshing from the sameness of some of the hotels.

Dinner was a scrumptious lamb, prune, and almond *tajine* in the elegant dining room with its traditional carved plaster motifs. After dessert, several Tuareg tribesmen in their deep blue robes appeared unannounced. One of them was playing a *guembri*, the traditional stringed instrument, while the others danced to the mesmerizing clanging of their metal *krakebs*. After a bit the musician and dancers insisted that the hotel guests join in, and everyone had a quite a Tuareg experience. After the workout, the hotel manager popped in and handed out cans of cold beer, and none were more grateful than the Tuareg.

We got to bed at about eleven and fell into a deep sleep from the fresh mountain air. At about 3 a.m., I realized that it had been years since I had eaten that many prunes in a single sitting. I also soon realized that I had violated my number one travel principle of leaving a little flashlight on the side table next to my bed. I grabbed the switch on the lamp on the side table and clicked. All I got was a mental flashback of the solar panels and generator that I saw near the hotel when we arrived early that afternoon. I realized that either by purpose or failure that the generator was off. On this mountaintop, far from civilization dark meant pitch dark. Now time was running out and I had to start scanning the walls with my hands, looking for any clues that might lead me to the toilet. Fortunately, my fingertips finally felt porcelain before an international incident occurred.

After our uplifting Tuareg experience, we backtracked out of the mountains and connected with the road between Agadir and Marrakesh. The road is wide, well-paved and cuts through some colorful hill country. Eventually we came upon the industrial outskirts of Marrakesh. We continued along bustling wide downtown streets. After fifteen minutes of passing modern rose colored apartment complexes, I had to pull over to get a better look at my map and catch my breath. Fortunately, we were just a few blocks from our destination, and I realized that most of the hotels that we were visiting were all in a short distance of *Avenue de President Kennedy* where we had pulled over. Suddenly Marrakesh seemed to shrink into a very manageable medium sized city comfortably surrounding the *medina*.

Our first hotel was the famous, historic La Mamounia. We pulled into its palm-lined driveway leading to the entrance. Military style gray coated bellhops were the first tip that the La Mamounia is a hybrid of European and Moroccan culture.

The La Mamounia was built in 1929 in the olive gardens that were said to have always existed at the heart of Marrakesh. At one time, the grounds were part of the palace of several generations of Marrakesh Sultans. The word Morocco is an Anglicization of the Arabic word *maraksh*. Today the gardens are a magnificent oasis of color and scent.

Throughout the 30's and 40's the La Mamounia was the hot spot for the rich and famous of Europe and the States. It still retains its iconic blend of Art Deco Moorish design that became a trademark of Paris and Hollywood in the 30's. It was here that Saharan mystique met European luxury. All the rooms were fitted with custom designed inlaid Deco furniture and replicas are in the rooms today.

There is one courtyard that rivals the Al-Hambra in Granada, Spain. The rooms all have a large comfortable balcony overlooking the gardens (or the famous Koutoubia Mosque on the other side.) Winston Churchill would come here during the winters to paint the gardens. It is said that this was his favorite hotel, and surely old Winnie had stayed in the best.

The elegant swimming pool has a small island with palm trees. For lunch we sat about the pool and indulged in the magnificent barbecue buffet, with its endless choices of salads, fish or fowl and deserts, both Middle Eastern and European.

Oddly there wasn't anyone in the pool. Everyone was just laying around the garden or pool under the warm Marrakesh sun. I wondered if the rich and famous were afraid to get their hairpieces wet. Anyway, I was not to be denied. I dove in, wanting to fully capture this magical moment. As my body started to shut down from the freezing temperature, I quickly realized why no one else was in the pool. Nonetheless, I was determined to experience this post card moment, even if it killed me. I feverishly paddled about thinking I might adjust; I didn't. I could see the all the sunbathers peering at me over their Pierre Cardin sunglasses, like I must have lost my mind.

I suspected that the French were probably thinking to themselves, "Phhhh, these stuupeed Germans, they are so insensitive that they can't even tell if the water is hot or cold."

I was thinking, "My God, $350 a night and they don't even heat the pool."

Had time and money allowed we could have spent weeks in the La Mamounia's courtyards and gardens, but we had neither and we wanted to visit the *medina* with the special mission of looking for Amazigh jewelry. We left the rental car in the parking lot and hired a taxi to shuttle us to various destinations in the *medina*. The taxi driver didn't disappoint us as he quickly pinpointed the premier jewelry, carpet, and brass work bazaars. We weren't shopping on this trip, however for us the bazaars are art galleries. Also, we wanted to get photos to include on our website.

We got to know the taxi driver a bit as he drove us around and we came to appreciate his sophisticated knowledge of Marrakesh, its history, and arts. So, when he invited us home to dinner we accepted. I can't imagine anywhere else where we would readily accept a dinner invitation from a taxi driver, but he called his wife, and he assured us that she was ready and willing to put on a Moroccan feast. Moroccan restaurants are superb, but nothing can compare to a home cooked Moroccan meal with its *couscous*, *tajines*, salads, breads, deserts, and legendary hospitality.

A couple of days later we took quick tours of a couple of new hotels outside of the city. The first was the Amanjena. It is one of the very exclusive and expensive resorts of the Aman chain of Malaysia. I was impressed by their success at capturing the less ornate, more natural form of Moorish design that is common to the *kasbahs* in the river valleys of the south. They made very effective use of many fine examples of Amazigh carpets of the region.

Nonetheless, there was a strange atmosphere that seemed somehow out of place. The female staff were all scarved and clothed in a tasteful vanilla colored fabric that was elegant but not very Moroccan. Nor was there anything resembling a typical reception desk. Then Louise, who was familiar with the Aman hotels, clued me in that these were Malaysian and not Moroccan women. I could stop trying to speak Arabic to them. Since I have just described how much I liked the Moroccan-European fusion at the La Mamounia, I suppose I shouldn't be too concerned about the Moroccan-Malaysian fusion at the Amanjena.

We also toured another impressive hotel in the '*Circuit de Palmerie.*' The Golf Palmerie is the polar opposite of the Amanjena. The lobby is an impressive tribute to traditional ornate Moorish interiors – intricately carved white plaster and hand chipped mosaic tiles. The high ceiling is made of intricately hand carved Islamic designs in dark wood. For all its elegance, the Golf Palmerie struck us as somewhat out of place. It is Palm Springs for Europeans.

One of the unusual hotels that we stayed in was the Es Saadi. It is well located, and like the La Mamounia, has a large garden with clay tennis courts and what a novel idea - they heat the swimming pool. In fact, the swimming pool is the main attraction at the Es Saadi. The pool is so close to the front desk, you almost fall in when you enter the lobby. The subliminal message is pretty clear – RELAX. The mostly European guests were dining around the huge pool in their swimsuits as white-coated waiters were buzzing around. It was almost as if someone had plunked a swimming pool with a palm tree island in the middle of a Parisian restaurant, and all the diners showed up in their bikinis and speedos.

After our inspiring stay in Marrakesh, it was time for our much-anticipated return to Fez. We checked out early and made the six-hour drive, arriving in the early afternoon. We knew things would be different as twenty-four years had passed since we had lived in Fez. We had expected wider roads and more traffic but were unprepared for the young men on motor scooters who dangerously swarmed around the car, shouting to us to follow them to this hotel or that. It was the same harassment as the old days, except in 2000 the tourists were beginning to show up in rental cars and the hustlers also had wheels. Fortunately, the road was well marked showing the directions to the major hotels. We had no need for a guide, at least not to just find our hotels.

Of course, it is essential to have a guide in the *medina* the first few times as you are certain to get lost and people don't always give you accurate directions. The major hotels have licensed government guides, and it is generally worth the money to know that you have an almost honest guide. Bear in mind of course that he may have his own agenda. He'll probably take you to his cousin's shop or at least someone with whom he has worked out a commission. Nor is it to his advantage to get you a good deal so don't give too much credence to his advice when it comes to making a purchase.

Our first night we stayed at the Jnan Palace - which is mostly a conference center for large European groups. It is on large grounds in the *Ville Nouvelle* (new city) with a huge swimming pool and is graced with lovely traditional Moroccan architecture. Louise was tired from the drive and just wanted room service before she got to bed early. I dined by myself as I needed to get photographs of the restaurant and other facilities. As I approached the elegant Moorish entrance to the restaurant, a young *Maitre D'* appeared and asked in English, "Are you lonely tonight?" I was rather taken back and for a moment didn't know exactly what to say. Then I realized he meant to ask if I was dining alone. I told him that my wife decided to eat in the room, but I had come to eat in the restaurant and take photos as had been arranged with the hotel manager. The *Maitre D'* seated me and called the manager. The manager was a friendly fellow, and he told the waiter to get me whatever I wanted and send him the bill. He then asked how I liked the hotel. I said it was wonderful but laughed and told him what the *Maitre D'* asked when I came into the restaurant. He also was quite amused but also wanted to make sure it didn't happen to a less understanding guest. He rounded up the waiters and told them the difference between 'alone' and 'lonely.' Two of the waiters started laughing, gave each other high fives and started singing Elvis Presley's iconic hit "Are you Lonesome Tonight?" They were really quite good, and we were all very amused that they happened to know this particular song.

The second night we moved to the Merinides - the infamous hotel that left my brother-in-law, Jim Grelle, wrapped in a towel in the hallway twenty-four years earlier. The hotel had been completely renovated after its own striking workers set torch to it during the Gulf War. (I accused Jim of casting a spell.)

We had a memorable stay. Our room had a wonderful balcony and since the Merinides is perched on a hill overlooking the *medina* the view was fantastic. That evening there was a full moon, and we spent an enchanted couple of hours peering down into the *medina*. Time had truly come to a halt. Not only had the last twenty-four years since we lived in Fez somehow melted away, so too had hundreds of years of history vanished in the blink of an eye. Rome may be the eternal city but not in the sense that Fez is. Fez is not a monument, it is a living, breathing medieval city.

The Merinides Hotel is owned by the Meridien hotel chain (the similarity of the names is coincidental.) Consequently, the Merinides had the exact same orange bedcovers and curtains as all the other Meridian hotels in Morocco. What's worse they were bright orange. Also, the prints were the same in each hotel. I was reminded of the little Kerdous with all its original paintings. Moroccan artists aren't all that expensive, nor are the hand-woven carpets and other crafts. There really is no excuse that a major chain of five-star hotels doesn't make more effort in this regard. Nonetheless, in fairness I should mention that the Merinedes' Moroccan restaurant was one of the better examples of Moorish architecture on the trip. Also, their international restaurant has floor to ceiling windows with a stunning view of the *medina*. Moroccans themselves like to come here for tea or orange juice and look at their ancient city. It is a great idea even if you are staying elsewhere.

Over the years we had unfortunately lost contact with Naima and as we were checking out of the Merinides I thought I should at least make a wild stab at making contact. I went over to the concierge desk.

"Excuse me Sir, I heard *concierges* know everything," I said.

"I do my best," he replied sensing he was about to get a zinger.

"I would like to find an old friend of ours. Her name is Naima Belghiti," I asked hopefully.

A big smile came to the *concierge's* face. "I know Naima and Drihany quite well, give me a moment and I will write down directions to their home."

He handed me the directions and I handed him a good tip. "I must say you certainly earned this one," I said still somewhat stunned at what had just transpired.

Given that Naima's husband had held a prominent position it is not surprising that he would be well known. Nonetheless, Fez was a city of a million people and the first person I randomly asked knew Naima and the directions to her house. It reminded me of when I returned to Fez twenty-four years earlier and found Naima locking up the Center for the last time.

Fortunately, Naima was home, and we had a great reunion. She was thrilled to introduce us to her twenty-three-year-old daughter whom we had never met. We talked about our trip and when she heard I would be in Casablanca the next week, she said she would be there as well and we could meet for coffee, which we did.

Our final night in Fez, we stayed at the Palais Jamai. The palace section of the hotel was built in 1879 by the Grand Vizir to Sultan Moulay Hassan. The Royal Suite and the Fassia Moroccan Restaurant were part of the old palace, and they give a glimpse of the splendor that the Fezi upper-class built at that time. The arches and ceilings are carved wood. Ornate, yet subtle, they are wonderful examples of the best of Moorish interiors.

The palace was turned into a hotel in 1939. A new section was later added and renovated just before our stay in 2000. The rooms are fine examples of how a hotel should use the local craftsmanship. The spacious balconies overlook the beautiful gardens and pool. There is a magnificent view of the *medina*, but it really looks up into the *medina*. The hotel is located at *bab jdeed*, one of the gates that is down at of the bottom of the *medina*, and you walk right out of the hotel into the *medina.*

Given that for four years I spent my weekends walking the *medina's* narrow alleys, I hoped that it would not be necessary to hire a guide to navigate the *medina*. The *medina* is organized into shopping districts or *souks*. Textiles shops were in one area, brass in another, and so on. Consequently, if you had a basic understanding of the layout, you had a fighting chance to find your way through the maze. But it had been twenty-four years since we lived in Fez, and we usually entered from other gates. How would we do?

The answer came quickly. We were walking uphill which meant we were basically headed to the center of the *medina*. We were in a residential area, so we continued. I was confident that I would see something familiar soon. Then we came upon some shops and some critical turns.

All eyes were watching, for various reasons but mostly to see if we really knew where we were going. In fact, I was now lost. I thought we were in striking distance, but I didn't want to spend the evening wondering around in circles. My left leg is impaired, I have a limited range, and I was using it up fast.

I approached a little shop selling cassettes. I made some small talk, bought a tape, and then quietly asked, "Which is the shortest way to the tomb of Moulay Idriss?"

You may remember, Moulay Idriss was the founder of Fez, and it was his tomb which I visited on my first day in Fez back in 1971. The man sympathetically nodded toward the alley to the left. We thanked him and continued, knowing that this wouldn't be the last time that we would need help.

Suddenly, a young boy of thirteen of fourteen appeared. I suspect that the man sent him after us. It used to be that each gate to the *medina* was crawling with these young lads offering their services as guides.

They called themselves "*Les petite guides.*" They often spoke several languages and would hang on to you pointing directions whether you needed them or not. You could only get rid of them with great effort and then they would become surly and insulting. The authorities made their activities illegal because they were cutting into the trade of the official government guides and generally giving Moroccan tourism a bad reputation.

The young man who had been sent after us was being ever so cautious to not appear to be a guide. He would walk ahead to a fork in the alleys and then nod in the direction which we should turn. I admired his skills in covert tradecraft and willingness to take us on as clients in the hopes of making a couple of bucks.

Along the way, Louise ducked into a nice little shop that had various antique artifacts. She picked out a couple of good-sized silver 'Hand of Fatimas.' Fatima was the only child of the Prophet Mohammed, and it is believed that her hand protects one from the evil eye. You will see this design throughout the Middle East. In Fez, you would not only see it as jewelry but also painted on the front door of homes and on the rump of horses and mules as well.

Finally, we arrived at the tomb of Moulay Idriss. I was somewhat reoriented now but not ready to abandon our little guide. We still needed to make it back to the hotel in the dark and I forgot to drop crumbs to mark my way back. There are candle *souks* near the shrine, and I purchased some candles as the *shawafa* had instructed me twenty-four years earlier. I had not sought out the services of a psychic since then, but neither was I inclined to ignore her sage advice. I also bought several loaves of bread for beggars sitting near the shrine.

Our little guide said nothing but was clearly taken back at how this lost tourist knew so much about the intimate customs of his city. A few of the shop owners asked him what I was doing, and word quickly spread from shop to shop about what this *nazarani* had just done. They seemed puzzled but approving.

The guide then asked, "Is that all you came to do?"

"No," I said "Let's go to a good carpet shop, real quality antiques, no junk." He smiled; now we were talking real money.

We were off again, with our young guide twenty yards ahead, occasionally circling back and saying we weren't far. Suddenly we ducked into a rather non-descript little door. I was at first taken back as it didn't look like an entrance to a very good carpet dealer. But once inside we realized it was a splendid old Fezi *riad* with high ceilings and balconies, now converted into a large bazaar overflowing with carpets. The owner told me that Jews lived in the building long ago, and he still had a few of their finer pieces. Then he was quick to add that he didn't discriminate against Jews or Christians. Who knows how deeply he felt this, but at least he was savvy enough not to offend a potential customer.

Louise was looking for some smaller carpet pieces. After eight years in Saudi Arabia, we had more carpets than we had floor space, so we weren't actively trying to buy anything. This was more ceremonial, like the candles and the bread – a commemoration of the good times we had doing business in Fez. We were the only customers and things preceded at a casual pace. The owner insisted on showing us some larger pieces just for interest. We sipped at our mint tea and then he finally started showing us some of his little jewels. One of the nicest was a small kilim with intricate detail. It had been woven by Jews who lived this neighborhood in the early 1920s.

You see, I don't discriminate against the Jews, they did very nice work," he said, apparently pleased to now have the proof in his hands.

We found three pieces that we liked - all very old and very fine craftsmanship. We bargained with him a bit, but I was not terribly concerned. His price was reasonable and surely he didn't have too many of this age and quality.

I got out my wallet and realized that I forgot to cash more travelers checks at the hotel before I left, and I was short $50 to $60. I pulled out my Visa Card and asked the man if he could take it. He said that he could but proceeded to scold me for being so willing to give out my number to just anyone.

"If you give your card to the wrong person, it will be all over the *medina* in an hour. It happens all the time here, you know," he advised.

I quickly slipped my card back in my wallet and he laughed that I now wouldn't give him the number. He was glad that I took his advice seriously. We talked about just getting two pieces, but he yelled up through the atrium to the second floor, and his pretty young accountant, and probably daughter, came down. He told her to go back to the hotel with us so we could cash some travelers' checks.

At the hotel, I took care of my business with the cashier and came back to where Louise was sitting. Louise said the bellhop threw the girl out because they thought she was a hooker. I was embarrassed and angry for her and myself. One would have thought that the bundles of merchandise would have made it self-evident that we had legitimate business with the young lady. I was reminded that in Morocco it is often the lower ranking employees that are the keenest on asserting caste. When we left the next morning, I told this same bellhop that I had given his tip to the lady accountant from the carpet shop. I think he got the message.

The next morning, we had a leisurely and delicious breakfast at Palais Jamais' elegantly tiled garden pool. In the distance, we could hear the faint clatter of craftsmen hammering out their designs in brass. It was pleasantly warm in the sun and a gentle breeze was rustling through the palm trees. It was difficult to once again wish farewell to beloved Fez, but it was hard to imagine a better last memory.

After breakfast we packed up and drove one hundred and twenty-five miles west to Rabat. It was not the familiar old road we used to take.

Instead, we were sailing along on a four-lane freeway. It was much like any American freeway except if I looked to either side of the freeway, I could see the old Morocco I knew and loved bumping along by donkey and cart. The impact of the new freeway was inevitable and there was no going back. Just as I had slipped into the Moroccan reality 25 years ago, Morocco was now traveling my American reality.

The Rabat Hilton is much like every other Hilton in the world, save its beautiful atrium café with tasteful Moroccan tile work. All quite nice, but we had been terribly spoiled by our recent stays at Fez's Palais Jamais and Marrakesh's La Mamounia, which were incomparably different experiences.

After a couple of days in Rabat, I took Louise to the airport in Casa, and she flew to the States via Paris. I spent that night at the Crowne Plaza. In many respects it was just your average innocuous modern hotel. After dinner I passed by the bar and a terrific Andalusian band was playing. I was the only one in the bar and I stayed up late listening to a fabulous performance. I probably drank a half dozen pots of mint tea and ate three plates of cookies. The band was thrilled that there was someone in the hotel who appreciated their music as much as I did, proving that it isn't necessarily the size of the audience that determines the quality of the performance. Likewise, a non-descript hotel can distinguish itself with great entertainment.

The next morning, I drove three and a half hours north to Tangier to see a couple more hotels. The freeway to Tangier was new, lightly traveled and equipped with great rest areas. It was now easy to tour Morocco, from south to north, up along the pristine Atlantic coast until it meets Mediterranean Sea at Cap Spartel outside of Tangier.

The coastline was still surprisingly underdeveloped, forested, and ripe for the right kind of tourist development. Morocco had been very patient in ensuring that new tourism development was of high quality and maintained the scenic atmosphere of the coastlines.

Despite my bad first day in Tangier years before, which I now accept as fate, I have come to appreciate the city a great deal. Tangier has a fascinating history, strategic importance, and enormous potential. For hundreds of years ships passed through the Strait of Gibraltar under the watchful eyes of the Tangerines. Not all the ships sailed by unscathed. This was especially true for Britain which had no alternative for their ships sailing to Italy, India, and the Middle East.

Likewise, all the overland traffic between Africa and Europe is channeled through Tangier and the Strait of Gibraltar. This has been particularly true for tourism in recent years with nearly a million French and over a half million Spanish coming to Morocco every year.

From 1912 to1956, Tangier was designated an international zone to keep the competing colonial powers from jostling for strategic position on the African side of the Strait. Other powers were determined that Spain did not have any more control of these strategic waters than it already possessed with its North African enclaves Ceuta and Melilla. In Tangier each of the powers had their own currency and postal services and the absence of tariffs spurred trade. There was a lively international community and Tangier became a rare and successful experiment in internationalism.

Its mystique and tax-free status attracted writers, artists, celebrities, and wealthy eccentrics. The Woolworth heiress Barbara Hutton kept a fabulous home in the *medina* and burned through her millions entertaining the visiting intelligentsia. The books and short stories of longtime resident American author Paul Bowles documented the era and added to the city's mystique - as though it needed any help.

It was a pirates' den turned intellectual Mecca - seedy, immoral - anything could be had and rather cheaply at that. The very name Tangier rings of drug dens and brothels, dark alleys, spies, and double agents. It is a reputation that will not die quickly.

Abdesalam often warned me, "Be very careful in Tangier, they are not like other Moroccans - they are bad people."

I do not like such stereotypes, but I had to admit that one of those 'bad people' had stolen my wallet.

Today Tangier is less sinister. The government has done a remarkable job of transforming the city into a modern hub of international industry and trade. Of course, this has come at the expense of some of its old-world mystique. Our big mistake on our initial visit in 1971 was that we were unprepared. We had no idea when we first got off the ferry that there was a more benign *Ville Nouvelle* (new city), where we could have adjusted to things more slowly. Instead, we went directly into the *kasbah* where we were overwhelmed by professional tourist hustlers looking for overwhelmed Westerners. When we went back a year later, instead of heading directly into the *kasbah*, we went east along the bay and found a charming small hotel with a lovely courtyard where we had breakfast among the palm trees. Then we would stroll along the *Ville Nouvelle's* boulevard and have cappuccinos at one the iconic outdoor cafes. Once we were in 'fighting shape,' we were ready to tackle the *kasbah*.

Today high-rise hotels line the beach along the bay. They are quality hotels with lovely views and easy access to the beach, nonetheless, I am grateful I experienced the Bay of Tangier in the days when smaller family-owned hotels lined the bay.

When I returned during our grand hotel tour in 2000, I stayed at the El Minzah Hotel. It was once the residence of a wealthy British gentleman. It is elegant, understated and a fine example of the Old Tangier. When I first drove up in front of the hotel, I thought that I must have had the wrong address. The small gothic entrance looks rather Greek and out of place on the ordinary street winding its way down to the harbor. The street was classic Tangier; everyone was watching my every move and offering me services I didn't want. I was reluctant to run into the hotel while my bags were still in the trunk, but I couldn't see where I had any choice.

At the desk I found a helpful clerk in a red fez standing at a small counter in a small lobby. He told me that the parking entrance was just down the street. I decided to forego checking in until my little rental Peugeot was safely out of reach of the several men scanning its contents. Once in the parking lot I started to think that perhaps I had come to the right place after all. The lot was full of black and dark blue Mercedes. I had to maneuver my humble rental back and forth to edge into a small slot, showing great care as to not run up a big bill in the parking lot before I even got to my room.

I went back to the lobby and produced my passport. As I was filling out the check-in-form, I started surveying the lobby more closely. Although small, the architectural detailing was superb. I was reminded that so often fine things come in small packages.

My room was nice but not especially memorable - until I opened the curtains and looked down into the pool and garden, then out across the rooftops to the glittering Bay of Tangier. I later saw one of the suites which had double glass doors that opened onto this memorable view. Indeed, I thought this IS the way to see Tangier. I reflected back on that $2 hotel twenty-nine years earlier on my first day in Tangier and reminded myself that one's impressions of a tourist destination have much to do with your means and method of approaching it.

From the lobby, there is a narrow artfully sculpted stairway that opens on to a large courtyard ringed with Moorish arches. The entrances to the restaurant, lounge and wine bar are off the courtyard. The bar and restaurant are a complete delight of multiple sculpted white arches. I sat in the bar for a while and quietly imagined the discussions that must have gone on between the likes of William Burroughs, Paul Bowles, Allen Ginzburg, Aaron Copeland, and other creative souls attracted to this inspiring location.

I decided to dine in the wine bar. Its small, intimate feel suited my mood. I sat at a table under a signed photo of Jacque Cousteau sitting at the very same table. He seemed to be asking, "Enjoying your fish, *mon ami?*" and indeed I was.

On my way out of town I drove up the Montagne, where the rich and royal keep their summer palaces. Malcolm Forbes' residence is now a museum. King Fahd of Saudi Arabia reportedly kept a palace here for a Moroccan wife. The view from the Montagne overlooks the city, the bay, the Strait of Gibraltar, and the southern tip of Spain.

A person of more humble means can get much the same view by continuing up to Cape Spartel. The drive up through the fragrant marine cedar trees is invigorating. You finally come out on a point with a vast sweeping view of the coastline down along the Atlantic. If you turn right, you head out to Cape Spartel at the very northern tip of Africa.

There was small cafe and a light house - a fantastic place for a cappuccino or two. I sat in the sun, listened to Segovia on my headset and stared off toward Spain. We used to come here in our van and camp. It was as though we were the only people on earth. The only thing that had changed was that the last two kilometers of the road had been allowed to crumble. How odd I thought; normally Moroccans were more conscious of their jewels. But here they seemed to have forgotten one of their greatest treasures.

After saying goodbye to Cape Spartel once again, I headed south along the coast to Asilah and caught up with the freeway down to Casa. I spent the night in a less expensive hotel and left early for the airport. Fortunately, before I flew out, I was able to meet Naima for coffee, as she was by chance visiting her sister Rashida. It would be the last time I would see her as she passed away recently. Naima was not only a wonderful person, but she was also a rock-solid business partner and a window for us to better understand Moroccan culture and mysticism.

The check-in for my flight back to Riyadh was a classic case of airline mismanagement. I got to the counter two hours early to avoid the mob scene. Things were going well until the ticket clerk showed up and started checking people in two gates down from where the sign for the check-in to Riyadh was hanging. That set off a panicked stampede with people at the end of the line suddenly becoming the front of the line. This was made worse by the fact that Arab women tend to travel with all their earthly possessions stuffed in huge suitcases. I finally spotted a dignified man in a red sportscoat walking through the terminal. I momentarily left my bags and ran after him.

"Excuse me Sir, are you with the airlines?" I asked. He said he was.

"May I ask a quick question?" He nodded.

"Would you look at the check-in to Riyadh over there. Now does that look more like an airline check-in or a food riot?" I asked rhetorically.

He laughed and told me to get my bags. Then he led me to the check-in for a flight to Tunisia which was empty and told the pretty young ticket agent to check me through to Riyadh. I was ever so grateful to be spared the airport scrum as my last memory of Morocco.

As the plane took off and banked east toward Saudi Arabia, I peered out my window and looked down upon Morocco from 30,000 feet. I reflected on the fact that despite my nearly fatal bout with brain cancer and years of skirting accidental death at the hands of Saudi drivers, I had indeed returned to Morocco for a third time, just as the *shawafa* had predicted, and I didn't even buy the airline ticket. I won it in a raffle at the Moroccan Ambassador's residence in Riyadh.

Morocco taught me many things, but nothing as profound as the power of fate - what the Arabs call *maktuub* (that which is written) While none but God truly know the future, it seems that some humans get little glimpses of things to come, no doubt just enough to keep us in a state of awe at this mysterious place called Morocco.

La Royal Mansour Hotel - Casablanca

La Mamounia Hotel - Marrakesh

Medina Salam Hotel - Agadir

Marrakesh Museum

Carved plaster

Medersa Bou Inania - Fez

Medersa Ben Youssef - Marrakesh

16 - PAINTINGS BY THE AUTHOR

Berber (Amazigh) Ladies

MOROCCAN MYSTIQUE

Amazigh (Berber) tents

MOROCCAN MYSTIQUE

Marrakesh Garden

MOROCCAN MYSTIQUE

Marrakesh Alley

Marrakesh Mosaic

El Jadida

Boujloud Gate - Fez

Amazigh (Berber) carpet *souk* (market)

MOROCCAN MYSTIQUE

Marrakesh Alley Sunset

MOROCCAN MYSTIQUE

Full Moon Over Chaouen

Fez Tile

Sous Valley

Oued Draa

MOROCCAN MYSTIQUE

Marrakesh

17 - ABOUT THE AUTHOR AND EDITOR

Bill - 1972

Louise - 1975

William (Bill) Keenan is an artist and graphic designer who lived in Morocco from 1971-74 and 75-76. He has an online art gallery based in Arizona. Louise Keenan is the business and media manager for the gallery. She lived in Morocco from 1975-76. The Keenans also lived in Saudi Arabia for nine years and in the United Kingdom for eight years.

Bill and Louise met as students at North Eugene High School in Eugene, Oregon in 1966. Bill studied graphic design at the University of Oregon and received an interdisciplinary master's degree at Portland State University. Louise received a master's degree in public policy at the University of Oregon.

Contact: bill@KeenanGallery.com

18 - ACKNOWLEDGMENTS

Our thanks go out to Ambassadors Christopher Ross and Kenton Keith, who provided me the employment and guidance that facilitated my four year stay in Morocco.

We are also forever grateful to friends and family who visited Morocco during our time there. Without that connection to home, it would not have been possible to continue our adventure as long as we did.

Special thanks to our business partners, Jim and Jean Grelle, and Bob and Christie Newland. Their support and willingness to engage in such an unconventional business adventure showed great courage and imagination. We wish it had been more financially successful, but success can also be measured in experiences, travel, adventure, and the satisfaction of knowing that you were fifty years ahead of your time.

Anyone who reads this book owes a special debt of gratitude to my wife and editor Louise, who took on the daunting challenge of transforming my scrambled memories into something readable.

Photo credits: Jennifer Godbold, Susan Morgan, Jim Grelle, and Christie Newland.

19 - GLOSSARY

The history of the Middle East and North Africa is quite long and at some point, pretty much everyone has invaded everyone else. Consequently, this led to a great deal of intermarriage, as well as cultural and religious overlap. That said, there are some useful generalities which give us a better understanding of the region, providing we don't lose sight of the complexities.

Berbers (Amazigh): the indigenous people of North Africa who have lived in the region since at least 10,000 B.C. The original Berbers were black Africans, who likely migrated from elsewhere in Africa tens of thousands of years ago. When the Romans invaded Morocco in 42 B.C., they named the country Mauritania, which means land of the Moors, or land of the black skinned people. Today the Berbers are considerably more racially mixed after two thousand years of successive occupations by Phoenicians, Romans, Vandals, Byzantines, Arabs, Spaniards, and the French. Consequently, Berber (Amazigh) is not a homogeneous race, but rather an ethno-linguistic culture of affiliated tribes across North Africa.

The term Berber comes from the Greek word barbaros, meaning barbarian, or basically anyone who didn't speak Greek. The Romans borrowed the term and applied it specifically to the indigenous tribes of North Africa. In any case, Berbers understandably regard the term as derogatory, so I use their preferred name from their native language, which is Amazigh (plural, Imazighen). Amazigh means 'free man' or 'man of the land.' As of 2021, an estimated 30% of Morocco's 37 million people spoke at least one of the three main dialects of the

Amazigh language, which is called Tamazight, an Afro-Asian language. In 2011, the Moroccan government recognized Tamazight as one of the country's official languages, along with Arabic and French, ending decades of trying to eliminate the Amazigh culture.

Arab: originally referred to the descendants of the tribes who lived on the Arabian Peninsula for thousands of years. Early scholars referred to this region as Arabia. At the time, Arab was most certainly an ethno-linguistic group, and one might argue a racial grouping as well. Many Arabs were nomads (Bedouins) and some tribes would migrate into desert areas as far north as present-day Syria, Iraq and Jordan in search of pastures for their goats and camels.

Djinn: according to the *Qur'an*, *djinn* (singular, *djinni*) are invisible beings made of smokeless fire, who inhabit a parallel dimension. *Djinn* can see humans, but humans can't see *djinn*, unless the *djinn* allow it. God is said to have created angels and *djinn* long before God created humans, however when God created Adam, God required *djinn* and angels to prostrate themselves to Adam, even though *djinn* have many powers that humans do not possess. God gave *djinn* magic, whereas God gave man intellect, apparently with the assumption that intellect is ultimately superior to magic.

Djinn supposedly can change from pure energy to physical forms like dogs, snakes, or humans. They can possess humans and some early Muslim scholars claim that in rare cases they have married humans and had children, although that was considered unlawful. Like humans, *djinn* have free will so there are necessarily good *djinn* and bad *djinn*; they are governed by the laws of religion and will be judged on Judgment Day just like humans. *Djinn* who accept the teachings of the *Qur'an* are permitted to attend mosque. Bad *djinn* are said to be jealous of humans because God made *djinn* prostrate themselves to humans. Consequently, they play various tricks on humans and use their powers of magic to get humans to prostrate themselves to the *djinn*, even though that is forbidden. The bad *djin*n are called *shayton*, which means devil in Arabic.

Of course, not all Muslims believe in *djinn*. Many contemporary Muslims scholars say Muslims are free to form their own opinions on the subject. These scholars believe the *Qur'anic* descriptions of *djinn* are likely metaphorical. For example, they argue that viruses and germs, which make people physically and mentally ill, were invisible to humans in the 7th century and might be the sort of thing to which the *Qur'an* was referring. Nonetheless, it is probably safe to say that most Muslims believe *djinn* wouldn't have their own chapter (*sura*) in the *Qur'an* if they did not exist.

Another interesting theory put forth by some contemporary Islamic scholars is that the *djinn* described in the *Qur'an* are likely the same phenomena as UFOs. These scholars point to the sightings of UFOs that appear as balls of fiery light that can shapeshift into various types of spacecraft. According to this theory: 'aliens' aren't necessarily extraterrestrials; they are more likely spirits from a parallel dimension; and what people have witnessed as UFOs could just be *djinn* performing magic tricks; alien abductions might be *djinn* possessing people; and UFOs might predate the existence of mankind and 'aliens' may have interbred with humans over the millenniums.

Gnawa: a sub-group of the Amazigh who were brought from Western Africa to Morocco as slaves and mercenaries by Sultan Ishmail bin Sharif in the 17th century. When they later gained their freedom, they were integrated into Amazigh tribes and Sufi Orders. Gnawa trance music integrates traditional Middle Eastern Sufi music with the African instruments, and rhythms and dance that the Gnawa brought from Western Africa. Gnawa music is said to have hypnotic mystical properties relating to healing, possession and other world experiences associated with *djinn*. In modern times, Gnawa music has been fused with jazz, electronic and popular music and now enjoys a worldwide reputation. An International Gnawa Music Festival is held every year in the southern coastal city Essaouira.

Muslims: are followers of Islam, the religion founded by the Prophet Mohammed in the early 7th century in what is present day Saudi Arabia. Soon after its founding, Islam spread quickly to the rest of the Middle East, as well as North Africa, southern Spain, and western India. At that time, Judaism and Christianity were already well established and not all of them converted to Islam, although over time most of them adopted Arabic as their primary language. To further complicate issues, the new converts to Islam and the Arabic language were often of different racial backgrounds than the original Arabs of the Arabian Peninsula. Nonetheless, today we define Arab as anyone whose mother tongue is Arabic and who lives in one of the twenty-two countries that make up the Arab League. Consequently, modern scholars no longer think of Arabs as being a race but rather an ethno-linguistic group that currently includes Caucasians and Africans. For example, by contemporary standards Amazigh may be included as a sub-group of Arabs because they speak Arabic and live in Arab countries. The Saudis, however, and with some justification, think of themselves and the rest of the native population of the Arabian Peninsula, as the 'real Arabs' and other Arabs are just 'Arab Lite.' Today 93% of Arabs are Muslim, but Arabs make up only 20% of the world's 1.5 billion Muslims. By far, the largest Muslim populations are in Indonesia, India, Pakistan, and Bangladesh.

Arab Muslims began their conquest of North Africa in the 7th century at the time of the Umayyad Caliphate, which had its capital in Damascus. The Amazigh, led by their legendary Queen Dihya, were initially successful in repelling the Arab advance. The resistance was in fact so successful that the Arab invaders called Queen Dihya *al-kahina*, which means sorceress in Arabic, as they supposedly believed her military successes were the result of her alleged ability to foretell the Arab military strategies. Many scholars think Arab generals simply claimed that Queen Dihya had special powers as way to rationalize their own tactical failures. Mystical powers or not, Queen Dihya was eventually defeated in the early 8th century, but her legend lives on as the symbol of the Amazigh resistance to Arab domination.

Semitic: We often hear the term anti-Semitic in reference to those who are prejudiced against Jews. Arabs are often accused of being anti-Semitic, which amuses them because Arabs also belong to the Semitic linguistic group. Today most scholars would argue that neither Arab nor Jew is a race, Judaism is a religion and ethno-linguistic group, while Arab is an ethno-linguistic group. There is also the matter, at least according to Scripture, that both Jews and Arabs, trace their ancestry to the Prophet Abraham. Regardless of whether that is historically accurate or not, that is what People of the Book (Jews, Christians and Muslims) more or less believe. Arabs are said to have descended from Abraham's son Ishmael, and Jews from his son Isaac. A recent DNA study supports the historical account which claimed that around 30,000 Jews were deported to Tunisia after the destruction of the Second Temple around 300 BC. It is likely that many Jews eventually migrated from Tunisia to Morocco, as did many Arabs.

Shi'a (Shi'ite) and Sunni: the two main divisions of Islam, a division that goes back to a controversy over who would lead the Muslim community after the Prophet Mohammed died in the 7th century. The Shi'a believed the Prophet's son-in-law Ali should have succeeded him. Whereas the Sunnis believed that a community consensus should decide the succession of Caliphs. Today, 85% of the world's 1.5 billion Muslims are Sunni, while in Iran 90% of the population are Shia. Only 0.1% of Moroccans are Shi'a.

Sufism: is a mystical form of Sunni Islam, some of whose practices made their way into Shi'ism as well. The most famous Sufi order is Turkey's whirling dervishes, however there is a wide variety of Sufi orders throughout the Sunni Muslim world. Some conservative Muslim branches believe Sufi practices are heresy, consequently at various times throughout history, Sufis have been subjected to oppression and purges. For their part, Sufis believe that Sufism is not a sect but an inherent, indivisible aspect of Islam.

Although less well-known than their Turkish counterparts, Moroccan Sufis also employ music, dance, chanting and meditation as means of achieving a trance like state in which the Sufi is said to be elevated beyond the ego and experiences the Oneness of the Divine. This of course is also the basic idea behind Zen Buddhism. Conservative Muslims argue that Sufis are committing heresy by trying to put themselves at the same level as God. Sufis refute that criticism by pointing out that when anyone gets past their own ego there is nothing left but the One (Allah). They do not claim to know all that God knows, they simply claim to understand God's most important message to man is that the material world is an illusion; all that is real is the cosmic love that binds all elements of the divine. Arguably that is the basis of all the great religions, although each claims to be the only true path.

Scholars generally say that Sufism arrived in Morocco in the 11th and 12th centuries and was spread from village to village by wandering aesthetics, many of whom would become regarded as saints for their piety, good works and reportedly in some cases miracles. Moroccan Sufis say that Sufism is indivisible from Islam as a whole, so Sufism necessarily came to Morocco when Arab Muslims first arrived in the early 9th century. The influence of Sufism in Morocco has ebbed and flowed over the centuries. At the time we were living in Morocco in the 1970s, the government was playing down Sufism because the government was working hard to give the country an image of modernity and Western scholars and younger urban Moroccan populations tended to view Sufism as backward and superstitious. Nonetheless, Sufism was deeply rooted in the culture, especially in rural populations, and the Sufis held on to their traditional beliefs and customs. There is also the matter that Moroccan Sufism incorporated many of the practices and traditions of the Amazigh, which is why it is often observed that Islam in Morocco has a distinctly African flavor.

After the 1992 Iraq invasion of Kuwait, the Arab World was divided between those who supported Iraqi leader Saddam Hussein and those who aligned with Kuwait and Saudi Arabia. In a bid to secure Moroccan support, the Saudis gave the Moroccans $5 billion in economic assistance. However, it came with the caveat that Morocco would allow Saudi Salafists (better known as Wahhabis) to proselytize Moroccans, especially the poor who would benefit from new mosques and social programs. Unfortunately, these Saudi religious entities had rather extreme beliefs and in some cases ties to al-Qaeda. Consequently, many young men in Casablanca's shanty towns were radicalized during the 90s.

After al-Qaeda's 2001 9/11 attacks and the 2003 Casablanca attacks, the King adjusted his policies regarding the Sufis. The choice was no longer seen as one between modernity or backward superstitions, rather it had become a choice between radical Islam or the Sufi emphasis on peace and tolerance. Morocco's Western allies have been strongly supportive of this approach to containing radicalism. Ties between Moroccan Sufi orders and those in West Africa were also strengthened in an effort to curb radicalism in those countries.

Moroccan Sufi culture has long been an attraction to Western tourists, so the government has begun to sponsor Sufi cultural and music festivals. Increasingly the Moroccan younger generation has blended Sufi music and dance with Afro-American hip-hop and rap, as well as electronic Deep House. This fusion has not only created a vibrant genre of popular music, but it has also likely ensured Sufism's relevance to younger Moroccans for decades to come.

MOROCCAN MYSTIQUE

Arabia - Nine Years In The Kingdom is the true story of William Keenan an American author, artist and Middle East analyst who lived in Saudi Arabia in the 1990s. He already had an academic background in Middle East and Arabic studies and had lived in Morocco for four years before moving to the Kingdom. However, he was eager to better understand how the traditional Bedouin culture was adapting to oil wealth and modernization.

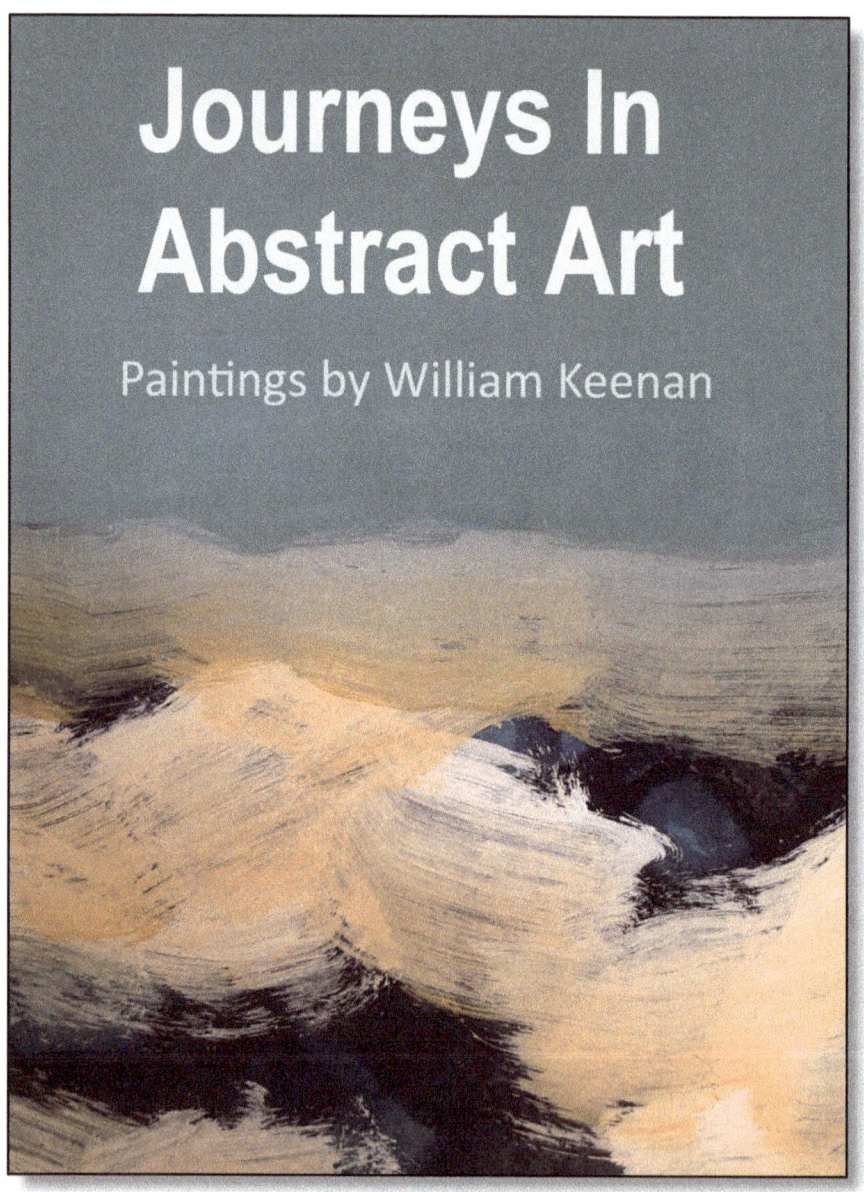

www.ingramcontent.com/pod-product-compliance
Lightning Source LLC
Chambersburg PA
CBHW050147170426
43197CB00011B/1997